PENTECOSTAL CLASSICS

Through the Bible Book by Book

Myer Pearlman

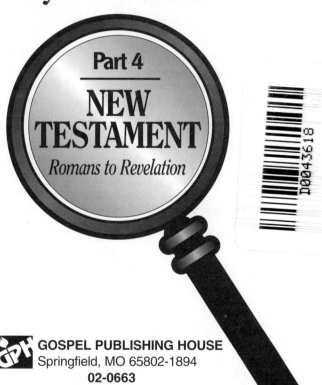

Part 4

NEW TESTAMENT

Romans to Revelation

GOSPEL PUBLISHING HOUSE
Springfield, MO 65802-1894
02-0663

20th Printing 2002

International Standard Book Number 0-88243-663-5

Printed in the United States of America

FOREWORD

The reader has, no doubt, watched a grocery salesman fill an order, and noted how well acquainted he was with the sections where the various articles were kept. This homely illustration will serve to describe the purpose of this course, which is to impart a general knowledge of the contents of each book of the Bible so that the Sunday school teacher with his lesson before him, may know from which of the sixty-six "compartments" of the Bible to select his material. This purpose has made necessary the method used in this course, which is not to deal primarily with details, but with the main facts of each book.

CHAPTER I

ROMANS

Theme. The epistle to the Romans is a complete, logical, inspired answer to the great question of the ages, "How should a man be just with God?" Job 9:2. In the Old Testament, the Gospels, and the Acts, are found scattered in different places teachings concerning that great doctrine which forms the very foundation of Romans—justification by faith. It has remained for the apostle Paul to gather up these teachings and adding thereto the special revelations vouchsafed unto him, to give us the most complete statement of doctrine found in the New Testament, embodied in an epistle which has been called "the cathedral of Christian doctrine." We shall sum up the theme of Romans as follows: The justification of sinful men, the sanctification of justified men, and the glorification of sanctified men, through faith and by the power of God.

Occasion and Reason for Writing. While at Corinth on his last visit there Paul met a Christian lady named Phoebe who was going to Rome. Rom. 16:1, 2. He took advantage of this circumstance to send by her a letter to the church there telling them of his coming visit and giving them a statement of the distinctive truths which had been revealed to him.

When Written. During Paul's last visit to Corinth. 2 Cor. 13:1; Acts 20:1, 2.

Contents. The epistle may be divided into the following three broad divisions:

1. **Doctrinal,** unfolding Paul's argument of justification by faith. Chs. 1 to 8.

2. **Dispensational.** Chs. 9 to 11. In chapters 1 to 8 and 12 to 16 Paul deals with the church. In chapters 9 to 11 he turns aside for a short while to speak about Israel and to show their relation to God's plan of salvation. This section answers the question, What place does the Jewish nation have in God's plan of salvation.

3. **Practical,** containing exhortations relative to Christian living. Chs. 12 to 16.

We shall use the following outline as the basis of our study:

    I. Condemnation. 1:1 to 3:20.

    II. Justification. 3:21 to 5:21.

    III. Sanctification. Chs. 6-8.

    IV. Dispensation. Chs. 9-11.

    V. Exhortation. Chs. 12-16.

I. Condemnation. Chs. 1:1 to 3:20.

Before beginning the study of Paul's main argument notice —

1. The salutation. 1:1-7.

2. The introduction (1:8-15), where Paul expresses his intention of visiting the Roman church.

3. The theme (1:16, 17). Verse 16 contains in brief the subject of the whole epistle. The Gospel is—(1) the power of God unto salvation, (2) to everyone that believeth, (3) to the Jew first, and also (4) to the Greek.

Paul now begins his great argument for justification by faith by laying down his first premise; namely, the whole world is guilty before God and under condemnation. He shows that—

1. The heathen are under condemnation (1:18-32), because, having had a revelation of God in the beginning (vv. 19, 20), they rejected it (v. 21). This rejection of the light led to spiritual ignorance (v. 22), spiritual ignorance led to idolatry (vv. 23-25), and idolatry led to moral corruption (vv. 26-32).

2. The Jew is under condemnation (Ch. 2).

Instead of being humbled by his knowledge of the law as he should have been, he has become self-righteous and critical, his self-righteousness blinding him to the fact that in the sight of God he is no better than the heathen who have not the law (2:1-16). In fact his knowledge of the law increases his condemnation and makes him more guilty than the heathen who have not had the light (2:17-29).

3. There is no difference between Jew and Gentile; both are under sin, without any hope of being justified by the works of the law or by any human means (3:1-20).

II. Justification. Chs. 3:21 to 5:21.

The last section concluded with a picture of the whole world guilty before God, shut up in the prison-house of sin, and awaiting the penalty of the law. From the human side there is no way of escape; it must come from the Divine side. The way of escape is now revealed—justification by faith. By justification we mean that judicial act of God whereby those who put their faith in Christ are declared righteous in His eyes and free from guilt and punishment. It may be illustrated by a judge's acquittal of a prisoner and declaring him innocent.

We shall notice in this section:
1. The fact of justification by faith (3:21-31). The Jew could not conceive of righteousness apart from the law. But since the law condemned instead of justified, it could not bring salvation. But now God reveals a righteousness which is **apart from the law,** a gift (v. 24), obtained by all who believe in Christ (v. 22), and made possible by His atoning death (v. 25). Because Christ died and paid the penalty of the law, God can be just and a justifier (v. 26); i. e., He can acquit a guilty sinner without setting aside the demands of His holy law.
2. Old Testament illustrations of justification

by faith (Ch. 4). By referring the Jew to his own Scriptures Paul shows him that the above named doctrine is not new. He first of all mentions Abraham. If any Jew would have a right to claim justification by his works it was Abraham, the "father of the faithful," the "friend of God." This patriarch was righteous in the sight of God; but this righteousness was by faith and not by works (vv. 1-3). David was "a man after God's own heart." He received this testimony not because of his own righteousness, for he committed many sins, but because of his faith (vv. 6-8).

  3. The results of justification by faith. 5:1-11.

  4. The security brought by justification by faith (5:12-21). Just as surely as union with the **first Adam** brings sin, condemnation and death, so surely does union with the **second Adam** bring righteousness, justification, and life.

III. Sanctification. Chs. 6 to 8.

In chapters 1-5 Paul has been dealing with **sins,** the outward manifestation of sin in our nature, and with the guilt following those sins. In chapters 6-8 he deals with **sin;** i. e., with the sinful nature itself. The first section speaks of our deliverance from the **guilt** and **penalty;** the second section, of our deliverance from the **power** of sin. The first deals with our **actions;** the second with our **nature**. Chapters 6-8 answer the question: now that he has been justified, what is the Christian's relation to sin? The answer to this question may be reduced to one word—Sanctification, i. e., separation **from** sin and separation **unto God.**

In this section we learn that—

  1. The Christian is dead to sin (Ch. 6). His baptism was symbolical of his identification with Christ in death and resurrection (vv. 1-10). The Christian by faith is to reckon himself dead to sin

(vv. 11, 12); and this reckoning finds its practical application in his turning from every known sin and his yielding to God (v. 13).

2. The Christian is freed from the law as a means of sanctification (Ch. 7). As death dissolves the marriage relation, so the believer's death to sin releases him from the law (vv. 1-6), that he might be married to Christ. This relationship to the law brought him constantly under condemnation, for it required a righteousness that corrupt human nature could not yield. This was not so much the fault of the law, for it was good, holy and spiritual. The fault lay with the carnal nature that could not fulfill its requirements. After describing his own experience when he discovered the spiritual nature of the law and his own inability to keep it, Paul utters a cry which is both a call for help and a question: "O wretched man that I am, who shall deliver me from the body of this death?"

3. The answer to this cry is found in chapter 8 where we learn that the righteousness which the law requires is worked out in us by the Holy Spirit who comes to dethrone sin, produce the fruits of righteousness, bear witness to our sonship, and help us in prayer.

IV. Dispensation. chapters 9 to 11.

So far Paul has been unfolding God's plan of salvation, and has come to the conclusion that salvation is by faith in Christ to all who believe, whether of Jew or Gentile. He has been dealing with salvation in relation to the **individual,** but what is its relation to Israel as a **nation?** If they as a nation have been rejected what becomes of the Old Testament promises of national restoration? If Israel is God's chosen people, to whom were committed His Word and to whom were given the covenants, and the law, why is it that they as a nation have rejected their Messiah? Will Israel ever be restored? What is to be the attitude of the Christians toward them? These questions are anticipated by Paul and are answered by him in the section we are about to study.

Let us sum up the contents of this section:

1. The theme of chapter 9:1-29 is as follows: Though the greater part of the Jewish nation have rejected Christ, yet God's promises concerning their national redemption have not failed, for within the nation there is a faithful remnant, who, when the time comes for Israel's complete restoration, will form the nucleus of the new nation.

2. The theme of chapters 9:30 to 10:21 is as follows: Israel's rejection is entirely their own fault.

3. The central thought of Chapter 11 is as follows: The rejection of Israel is neither total nor final. It is not total for there is a remnant of the nation who are true to God and their salvation is a pledge of the salvation of the entire nation (vv. 1-10). It is not final, for after that the fullness of the Gentiles has come into the church, God will send the Redeemer who shall bring the entire nation into that condition of Millennial blessedness and glory foretold by the prophets (vv. 11-36).

V. Exhortation. chapters 12 to 16.

Like most of Paul's doctrinal epistles, Romans contains a practical section. The apostle may carry his readers to the highest heights of Christian doctrine, but he never fails to bring them back to earth where they are to apply the doctrine to daily life. The above section really follows chapter 8. Chapters 9-11 are parenthetical; i. e., they are inserted because of their great importance, but are not necessary to complete the sense of the epistle. Romans would be complete—at least **in form**—without these chapters. The "therefore" of 12:1 is the link that connects this section with the first eight chapters. Because of what has been set forth in those chapters—their justification, sanctification and hope of coming glorification—Christians are to consecrate themselves to God, serve one another in love, and walk in wisdom and holiness before the world. We shall sum up the contents of this section as follows:

1. The Christian's duty as a member of the church (12:1-21): consecration (vv. 1, 2); service (vv. 3-8); love to the brethren (vv. 9-21).

2. His duty as the member of the state (13:1-7): obedience to authority.

3. His duty toward other members of the state (13:8-14): love.

4. His duty toward weaker brethren (14:1 to 15:13): forbearance.

5. Conclusion (15:14 to 16:27). Paul's ministry among the Gentiles (vv. 14-21); his proposed visit (vv. 22-33); salutations (16:1-23); benediction (vv. 24-27).

Learn the following chapter outline of Romans:

Chapter
1. The heathen's guilt.
2. The Jew's guilt.
3. Universal condemnation.
4. Justification by faith.
5. Results of justification.
6. Freedom from sin.
7. Freedom from the law.
8. Freedom from condemnation.
9. The election of Israel.
10. The rejection of Israel.
11. The restoration of Israel.
12. Consecration.
13. Duties to the state.
14. Duties to weak brethren.
15. Paul's labor and coming visit.
16. Salutations.

CHAPTER II

FIRST CORINTHIANS

Theme. The epistle was written for the purpose of correcting disorders that had arisen in the Corinthian church, and of setting before the believers a standard of Christian conduct. We may therefore state its theme as follows: Christian conduct in relation to the church, the home and the world.

Why Written. Paul visited Corinth on his second missionary journey. (Compare Acts Ch. 18.) While at Ephesus, he heard of disorders that had broken out in the Corinthian church, and it is believed that he made a hurried visit to Corinth at that time. (This visit is inferred from the statement in 2 Cor. 12:14 that he was about to visit them a third time. The first visit was made during his second missionary journey, and the last, after writing 2 Corinthians.) After returning to Ephesus, he wrote them an epistle (now lost) instructing them as to their attitude toward sinning members of the church 1 Cor. 5:9. Later members of a Corinthian family visited Paul and informed him concerning divisions that had broken out in the church. A reply came to Paul's first letter (7:1) making certain inquiries relative to Christian conduct. To correct the disorders that had broken out, and to answer the inquiries, Paul wrote his first epistle to the Corinthians. We may thus sum up Paul's purpose in writing this epistle:

1. To correct the following disorders:
    (1) Divisions.
    (2) Immorality.
    (3) Disputes among saints.

(4) Disorders during the Lord's Supper.

(5) Disorders during worship.

2. To answer the following questions:

(1) Concerning marriage.

(2) Concerning the eating of meats offered to idols.

(3) Concerning the gifts of the Spirit.

When Written. At the close of Paul's three years' residence at Ephesus (Acts 20:31; 1 Cor. 16:5-8).

Contents

I. Correction of Social and Moral Disorders. Chaps. 1-8.

II. Apostolic Authority. Chap. 9.

III. Church Order. Chaps. 10-14.

IV. The Resurrection. Chap. 15.

V. Conclusion. Chap. 16.

I. Correction of Social and Moral Disorders. Chs. 1 to 8.

Under this head we shall study the subjects contained in the following outline:

1. Introduction. 1:1-9.

2. Divisions. 1:10-16.

3. The wisdom of God and the wisdom of man. 1:17 to 2:16.

4. Christian ministers, their relation to each other and to believers. **Chs. 3, 4.**

5. Immorality. Chap. 5.

6. Saints at law. 6:1-8.

7. The sanctity of the body. 6:9-20.

8. Marriage. Ch. 7.

9. Concerning meats offered to idols. Ch. 8.

Paul denounces the divisions existing among the Corinthians. The party spirit had well-nigh destroyed Christian love. The Corinthians possessed with an undue admiration for human leadership, had ranked themselves under the names of the different ministers, whom they attempted to set up against one another as rival leaders. Some admired the zeal and power of Paul; others saw in the cultured Apollos the ideal preacher; others belonging perhaps to the Judaizing party, held up Peter, the apostle to the Jews, as the model leader; others again, evidently discouraged by these divisions, styled themselves simply followers of Christ (1:12).

Paul devotes quite a large section to a comparison of God's wisdom and man's wisdom, and to a demonstration of the inability of the latter to reveal the things of God (1:17 to 2:1-16). His rebuke and renunciation of mere human wisdom and philosophy will be understood when we consider the Greeks had a profound admiration for learning and culture, and that there was a danger of their reducing Christianity to a merely intellectual system, and of making it one of the many schools of philosophy that existed in their country. It was this very love of human wisdom that had led to an undue regard for human leadership, and that, in turn, had resulted in divisions among them.

In chapters 3 and 4 Paul strikes at the root of the matter by clearly showing the ministers' relation to God, to one another and to the people.

While the Corinthians were glorying in their intellectuality, and were divided over leadership, they were all tolerating in their midst immorality of the basest kind (5:1-2). Paul, using to the full his apostolic authority (see Matt. 16:19; 18:17, 18), excommunicates the offender (that is, cuts him off from communion with the church), and delivers him over as it were, to the chastening hand of Satan (compare Job 1:12; 2 Cor. 12:7), in order that he might be brought to repentance (v. 5). From the second epistle to the Corinthians we learn that this man did repent. 2 Cor. 2:6-8.

Some of the Corinthians had been exposing the cause of Christ to reproach because of their going to law with one another before unbelieving judges (6:1-8). Paul tells them plainly that if they are to reign with Christ and judge the world and even angels, they should be able to judge their own cases and settle their own disputes

The words found in chapter 6:9-20 are directed against a class of people known in church history as Antinomians. These were professed believers, who, going to the other extreme from legalism, declared themselves free from the law altogether. From certain of Paul's statements to the effect that believers are not under law, and that they are not justified by any external observances, these heretics had falsely inferred that all outward acts were indifferent and one could be criminal. In refuting this error, Paul emphasizes the sanctity of the body.

In chapter 7 Paul answers an enquiry from the Corinthians concerning marriage. In studying this chapter it should be remembered that all the statements contained therein are not made by way of commandments (7:6), but many of them are the suggestions of a Spirit-guided man, who is viewing marriage in relation to local conditions in Corinth (the prevalence of immorality, 7:1), and in relation to coming persecutions of the church (vv. 26-29). It should be noted also that this chapter does not contain all of the New Testament teachings on marriage. For a complete study of the question, all the N. T. scriptures on the subject should be investigated.

Chapter 8 deals with the question of Christian liberty. Some of the Corinthian believers, who had been saved from heathenism, felt free in their conscience to accept invitations to feasts in idol temples, for, reasoned they, "An idol is nothing in the world, and there is none other God but one" (8:4).

Paul acknowledged these reasons, but warns the last-named believers that there were weaker Christians who were not acquainted with those facts, and who would be stumbled and fall into sin if they saw an enlightened believer eating in an idol temple.

II. Apostolic Authority. chap. 9.

In this chapter Paul defends himself against a small section of the church who were denying his authority as apostle (9:1-3). One of their charges was that he was not asking for financial support because he lacked authority to do so. Paul mentions as proof of his apostleship the fact that he had seen the Lord (v. 1), and refers to them as a church as the fruit of his ministry (v. 2). He claims equal authority with other apostles (vv. 4-6). He proves that he, as a minister of the Gospel, has a right to financial support, by a natural illustration (v. 7), by a quotation from the law (vv. 9, 10), by an illustration from the temple (v. 13). Then he tells why he has not availed himself of this right: he did not wish to hinder the Gospel by becoming a burden to the people (v. 12, compare 2 Thess. 3:8, 9); the fact of his preaching the Gospel without price was his reward (v. 18); in preaching the Gospel he considered himself simply an "unprofitable servant" (v. 16, compare Luke 17:10), for he was but doing his duty (v. 16). Paul is willing to forego his rights and adapt himself to all conditions, and to all classes of men in order that he might save a few souls (vv. 19-23). He has a good reason for making these sacrifices. For as Greek athletes, during their period of training, denied themselves many pleasures and comforts and subjected themselves to hardship in order to win a crown of leaves, so he was willing to make sacrifices in order to win an imperishable crown. (vv. 24-27).

III. Church Order. Chs. 10 to 14.

Under this heading we shall study the following subjects:

1. A warning against falling from grace. 10:1-13.

2. Christian liberty and idolatry. 10:14-33.

3. Conduct of women in assemblies. 11:1-16.

4. Disorders during the Lord's Supper. 11:17-34.

5. The gifts of the Spirit, their diversity and distribution. Chap. 12.

6. The spirit that is to regulate the use of these gifts. Ch. 13.

7. The rules for their regulation in assemblies. Ch. 14.

Though the Corinthians have been partakers of great spiritual blessings and have been recipients of the grace of God, Paul warns them that there is a possibility of their falling from their high spiritual standing. He proves this by a comparison of them with Israel.

In Chapter 10:14-33 Paul continues the subject dealt with in chapter 8; namely, Christian liberty in relation to the frequenting of heathen feasts. To those Christians who felt free to attend heathen feasts (compare 8:10), Paul utters a warning against falling into the snare of idolatry. Though Christians might feel free to indulge in some liberties, they are to consider whether such indulgences make for edification of believers as a whole (v. 24). When purchasing meat in a market, Christians are not to enquire whether the meat has been offered to idols, in order to avoid any unnecessary disturbance of their conscience (v. 25). But if a Christian accepts an invitation to dine with a heathen acquaintance, and he is told that the meat served has been offered to idols, he is not to touch it, for to partake of it under those circumstances would make it appear that he was condoning idolatry, and his action would be a stumbling block to many (27-29).

Chapter 11:1-16 deals with conduct of women in assemblies. On the surface, the verses seem to deal with the question as to whether or not a woman should wear a veil in church. But reading deeper, we discover that they deal with the God-ordained relationship of the woman to the man. Verse 3 seems to be the key verse to this section. In Paul's day, women wore a veil as a symbol of their subjection to the man. The Gospel had given women a liberty they had never realized before, abolishing in regard to salvation and standing in grace, the distinction of the sexes. Gal. 3:28. It seems that on the ground of this liberty, the Corinthian women claimed equality with the man in every respect, and as an open declaration of this claim, came forward to prophesy and pray without the veil. In so doing, they violated the divine order which is as follows: God is the head of Christ; Christ, of man; and man, of the woman (v. 3).

The remaining verses of this chapter deal with disturbances in the Lord's Supper. It seems that, before partaking of the Lord's Supper, the believers partook of a common meal together, commonly known as the love feast. During the last-mentioned feast many of the Corinthians had yielded to gluttony and drunkenness (vv. 20-22), with the result that they were not in a fit condition to partake of the Sacrament. After explaining the sacredness and significance of the Lord's Supper (vv. 23-26), Paul warns the Christians against partaking of it unworthily (vv. 27-29), lest they fall under divine chastisement (vv. 30-32).

Chapters 12, 13, 14 deal with the subject of spiritual gifts. Chapter 12 treats of the diversity and distribution of the gifts; chapter 13, of the spirit that should characterize their use; chapter

14, of the rules regulating their manifestation in the assembly.

IV. The Resurrection. Chap. 15.

Chapter 15 is the great resurrection chapter of the Bible. Paul was compelled to treat the doctrine of the resurrection in a fairly thorough manner, for there had been a denial of this doctrine. Some perhaps, misunderstanding Paul's teaching concerning the spiritual resurrection of the sinner had thought of this as the only resurrection; others possibly, belonging to the antinomian party (see notes of Chap. 6:9-20) did not care to look forward to the resurrection of a body which they had abused by sins of impurity.

V. Conclusion. Chap. 16.

We shall sum up the contents of chapter 16 as follows:

1. Concerning the collection for the needy Jewish saints. vv. 1-4.

2. Concerning Paul's intended visit. vv. 5-9.

3. Concerning Timothy's visit to them. vv. 10-11.

4. Concerning Apollos. v. 12.

5. Exhortations and greetings. vv. 13-24.

In order to impress the contents of 1 Corinthians on his mind, let the student memorize the following chapter outline:

Chapter

1. Divisions.
2. Wisdom of God and wisdom of man.
3, 4. Ministers.
5. Immorality.
6. Saints at law.
7. Marriage.
8. Christian liberty.
9. Apostolic authority.

10. Idolatry.
11. Lord's Supper.
12. Gifts.
13. Love.
14. Disorders in worship.
15. Resurrection.
16. Salutation.

SECOND CORINTHIANS

Theme. Of all Paul's epistles, 2 Corinthians is the most personal. It is a revelation of his heart, of his innermost feelings and deepest motives. This baring of his heart was not a welcome task to the apostle, but rather a reluctant one. The presence of false teachers at Corinth, who were questioning his authority, impugning his motives, and undermining his authority, had made it necessary for him to defend his ministry. In making this defense, he was compelled to relate experiences about which he would rather have been silent; and through his epistle he is careful to inform his readers of this fact. Bearing in mind that 2 Corinthians is Paul's personal vindication of his ministry, we will sum up its theme as follows: Paul's ministry, its motives, sacrifices, responsibilities and effectiveness.

Occasion for Writing

1. After writing the first letter at Ephesus, Paul went to Troas, where he waited for Titus to bring him an answer from Corinth (2 Cor. 2:13).

2. Disappointed in his expectation, Paul went to Macedonia where he met Titus who brought him news that the church as a whole had responded to his exhortations, but that there was a small minority that refused to acknowledge his authority.

3. To comfort and encourage the former, and to threaten the latter, Paul wrote his second letter.

Why Written

1. To comfort the repentant members of the church.

2. To warn the rebellious minority.

3. To warn against false teachers.

4. To resist the attacks made on his ministry by these false teachers.

Where Written

Probably at Philippi, during the third missionary journey.

Contents. The book is exceedingly difficult of analysis. As one writer puts it, "It is almost impossible to analyze this letter, as it is the least systematic of Paul's writings. It resembles an African river. For a time it flows smoothly on, and one is hopeful of a satisfactory analysis, then suddenly there comes a mighty cataract and a terrific upheaval, when the great depths of his heart are broken up." We shall divide the book into four sections, as follows:

I. Backward Glance. 1:1 to 2:13.

II. The Dignity and Effectiveness of Paul's ministry. 2:14 to 7:1-16.

III. The Collection for the Needy Saints of Judea. Chs. 8, 9.

IV. Paul's Vindication of His Apostleship. 10:1 to 13:14.

I. The Backward Glance. 1:1 to 2:13.

1. God sustains Paul in tribulation in order that he may in turn comfort others. 1:1-11.

2. My motives are pure! 1:12-14.

3. Why Paul delayed his visit. 1:15 to 2:11.

4. Paul's anxious waiting for news from Corinth. 2:12, 13.

II. The Dignity and Effectiveness of Paul's Ministry. Chaps. 2:14 to 7:1-16.

1. Paul's triumphs in the Gospel. 2:14-17.

2. Paul defends himself against the Judaizers and shows that the New Covenant is better than the Old. 3:1 to 4:6.

3. In sickness, danger, and persecution Paul's strength comes from the power of God and the hope of eternal life. 4:7 to 5:10.

4. The secret of Paul's earnestness is his sense of responsibility to Christ. 5:11-21.

5. Paul defends his faithfulness in preaching the Gospel. 6:1-13.

6. Be ye separate! 6:14 to 7:1.

7. Paul pleads with his converts to ignore the malicious and untruthful reports about him. 7:2-4.

8. Why Paul waited for Titus. 7:5-16.

III. The Collection for the Jewish Saints. Chaps. 8 and 9.

1. Remember the example of the poor Macedonians and above all the example of Jesus! 8:1-15.

2. Paul commends the bearers of the funds. 8:16-24.

3. Be ready to give liberally and so reap God's blessing! Chap. 9.

IV. Paul's Defense of His Apostleship. Chaps. 10 to 13.

1. Paul contrasts himself with false teachers. 10:1-18.

2. Bear with one who loves you! 11:1-6.

3. Why Paul did not ask for support. 11:7-15.

4. Divine signs and visions, faithful service and sufferings, prove Paul's right to apostleship. 11:16 to 12:13.

5. Please do not make it necessary for me to use my power to discipline you! 12:14 to 13:10.

6. Conclusion. 13:11-14.

CHAPTER III

GALATIANS

Theme. The question as to whether the Gentiles were to keep the law of Moses had been settled at the council at Jerusalem. The decision was that the Gentiles were justified by faith without the works of the law. But this decision did not seem to satisfy the Judaizing party, who still insisted that though the Gentiles were saved by faith, their faith was perfected by the observance of the law of Moses. Preaching this message of the mingling of law and grace, they did their utmost to turn Paul's converts against him and against the message he preached. In this they succeeded to the extent of bringing under the bondage of the law the whole church of the Galatians—a Gentile church. To restore this church to their former standing in grace, Paul wrote his epistle to them, the theme of which is, Justification and sanctification are not by the works of the law, but by faith.

Occasion for writing. Passing through Galatia on his second missionary journey, Paul was detained on account of sickness. Acts 16:6; Gal. 4:13. He was well received by the Galatians, and established a church there. Gal. 1:6; 4:14. While in Greece on his third missionary journey (Acts 20:2), he received the news that the Galatians had taken upon themselves the yoke of the law. This led to the writing of his epistle.

Why Written

1. To oppose the influence of the Judaizing teachers who were attempting to undermine Paul's authority.

2. To refute the following errors that they taught:

(a) Obedience to the law mingled with faith is necessary to salvation.

(b) The believer is made perfect by the keeping of the law.

3. To restore the Galatians who had fallen from grace.

When Written. During Paul's third missionary journey.

Contents

I. The Apostle of Liberty. Chaps. 1, 2.
II. The Doctrine of Liberty. Chaps. 3, 4.
III. The Life of Liberty. Chaps. 5, 6.

I. The Apostle of Liberty. Chaps. 1, 2.

In the first two chapters, Paul defends himself against the following charges made against him on the part of the Judaizers.

1. They denied that he was a true apostle of Christ, for he had not, like the Twelve, received his commission personally from the Lord.

2. They claimed that he was only a teacher sent out by the apostles, therefore his teaching should be accepted only as it agreed with theirs.

3. They charged him with spreading teachings not approved by the council at Jerusalem.

Notice how Paul answered these charges:

1. In the very first verse of the epistle, Paul emphasizes his divine commission as apostle. He then greets the believers (2-5). Notice there is an absence of the thanksgiving that characterizes his other epistles, for he is writing to a church which has fallen from grace. He is amazed that they have so soon turned from the true Gospel to what he terms a different gospel (v. 6); yet this **different** gospel is not **another** gospel, for there is but one; but this message they have obeyed is a perversion

of the gospel (v. 7). Upon those who would preach a different gospel he pronounces a curse (vv. 8, 9).

2. In verses 10-24 he refutes the charge that he received his teaching and commission from the apostles. He received them from the Lord Himself.

3. In chapter 2:1-10, Paul shows that his ministry and message were endorsed by the leaders of the church council at Jerusalem. Fourteen years after his conversion, Paul went to Jerusalem to attend the council and there defended his preaching of the justification of the Gentiles by faith alone (2:1; compare Acts 15:1, 2).

4. Instead of the Twelve finding fault with Paul, as had been charged, Paul affirms that he found fault with one of their number (2:11-21). After his vision (Acts 10:11-16), and his experience at Cornelius' house Peter cast off his Jewish prejudices and mingled freely in social intercourse with the Gentiles. But when certain of the strict Jewish Christians came from Jerusalem, who evidently looked with a criticizing eye on his conduct, (and those Jews with him) he separated himself from the Gentiles (vv. 11-13). This course of action Paul condemned as a cowardly compromise.

II. The Doctrine of Liberty. Chaps. 3, 4.

Paul rebukes the Galatians for turning from the truth of justification by faith, and tells them that their spiritual experience had no connection with their observing the law (3:1-5). He then takes up the argument that justification is by faith, apart from the works of the law (3:6 to 4:7). The following are its main points.

1. Even Abraham, the friend of God, was not justified by his works, but by his faith (v. 6). So that instead of the observers of the law of Moses being the children of Abraham (Compare Matt. 3:9), it is those who are justified by faith who can claim that right (v. 7).

2. The covenant that God made with Abraham was a covenant of **faith** (vv. 8, 9). This has no connection with the Mosaic covenant which was a covenant of **works** (v. 10). The Abrahamic covenant was made first; but the law, with its curse was added, and so blocked the way for the blessing of Abraham to come to the world. But Christ by His death removed the curse of the law (v. 13), so that the blessing of Abraham might come upon the Gentiles as well as the Jews (v. 14).

3. Paul then explains the relation between the Abrahamic and Mosaic covenants (3:15-18). If the blessing of Abraham is to come by the works of the law, then reception of that blessing is **conditional** upon keeping the law; but the covenant made with Abraham is **unconditional** (v. 18). The inference from the last verse is that if it is by the keeping of the law that the blessing of Abraham is to come upon the world, then that blessing will never come; for no one can be justified by the law.

4. Paul now explains the purpose of the law and its relation to the believer (3:19 to 4:7). Paul's foregoing arguments call forth the question on the part of the Jew, If the law cannot save why then did God give it to man (v. 19)? The Abrahamic covenant promised salvation through faith without the works of the law. But how could God teach man that salvation was only by faith, and not by any effort on his part? Only by placing him under law and showing him that his sinful nature could not keep perfectly its precepts, thus shutting him up to faith as a means of salvation (v. 19). The law does not stand in opposition to the Abrahamic covenant, for it was never intended to save man (v. 21); it was given to educate man to his need of salvation by faith (vv. 22, 23). Paul pleads with them to return to the full liberty of the Gospel. 4:8-31.

III. The Life of Liberty. Chaps. 5, 6.

This section may be summed up by the following exhortations:

1. Hold fast to the liberty of grace for the law cannot save you. 5:1-6.

2. Turn away from the false teachers who have perverted the Gospel and made you slaves to legalism. 5:7-12.

3. Though free from the Mosaic law, you are not free to sin. Walk in love and you will thereby fulfill the law. 5:13, 14.

4. You will be tempted though by the lower nature, but obey the promptings of the Spirit and you will be victorious. 5:16-26.

5. Bear one another's burdens, and be patient with the erring. 6:1-5.

6. Be mindful to support your ministers and you will thereby reap the Divine blessing. 6:6-10.

7. Conclusion (6:11-18). Beware of the Judaizers. I know quite well that they desire to win you simply in order to get a reputation for zeal. Glory only in the Cross in which alone there is real salvation.

EPHESIANS

Theme. For depth and sublimity of teachings, Ephesians stands supreme among all of Paul's epistles. It has been "Paul's third heaven epistle," "for he soars from the depths of ruin to the heights of redemption"—and "the Alps of the New Testament," for "here we are bidden by God to mount step by step, until we reach the highest possible point where man can stand, even in the presence of God Himself." The epistle to the Ephesians is a great exposition of a fundamental doctrine of Paul's preaching, namely, the unity of all the universe in Christ, the unity of Jew and Gentile in His body, the church, and God's purpose in that body for time and eternity. The epistle is divided into two sections: doctrinal (Ch. 1-3) and practical (Chs. 4-6). In the first section Paul sets forth the grandeur and glory of the Christian's calling; in the second he shows what should be the conduct of the Christian in view of this calling. In brief he teaches that a holy calling demands a holy walk. "He calls upon his readers to rise to the highest dignity of their calling, and as he does so, there emerges a picture of the church as a body predestined before the ages, to unite Jew and Gentile together, which, through the ages to come has to exhibit before the universe the fullness of the Divine life, living the life of God, imitating God's character, wearing God's armor, fighting God's battles, forgiving as God forgives, educating as God educates, and all this that it may fulfill the wider work whereby Christ is to be center of the universe." We shall sum up the theme as follows: the Church is chosen, redeemed, and united in Christ; therefore the Church should walk in unity and in newness of life, in the strength of the Lord and by the armor of God.

Why Written. There were two dangers that threatened the church at Ephesus: a temptation to sink to heathen standards; and a lack of unity between Jew and Gentile. To offset the first danger, Paul sets forth the holiness of the Christian's calling in contrast with their former sinful condition as heathen. To guard against the second, he presents the Lord Jesus as making peace between Jew and Gentile by the blood of His cross, and making of the twain a new body.

When Written. During Paul's first imprisonment at Rome. It was sent by Tychicus who also bore letters to the Colossians and to Philemon.

Contents. The student will notice as he studies

the outline with its main divisions and subheads, that the epistle yields itself to an arrangement in triplets, as suggested by Dr. Riley in his book "Ephesians the Threefold Epistle."

Doctrinal Section: The Church's Calling. Chs. 1-3.

I. The threefold source of our salvation. 1:1-18.

II. The threefold manifestation of God's power. 1:19 to 2:22.

III. A threefold statement concerning Paul. Ch. 3.

Practical Section: The Church's Walk Chs. 4-6.

I. A threefold exhortation to the whole church. 4:1 to 5:21.

II. A threefold exhortation to the family. 5:22 to 6:9.

III. A threefold expression of spiritual life. 6:10-24.

DOCTRINAL SECTION: THE CHURCH'S CALLING. CHS. 1-3.

I. The threefold source of our salvation. 1:1-18.

Our salvation, which is the sum of all blessings, finds its source in:

1. Predestination by the Father, who chose us before the foundation of the world to be His children and to be without spot or blemish. 1:4-6.

2. Redemption by the Son, through whom is given unto us a knowledge of God's eternal plan for the universe, and an eternal inheritance. 1:7-12.

3. Sealing by the Spirit, which is an earnest—a first payment—of the complete redemption which will be ours in the future. 1:13-14.

Paul utters a prayer that the Ephesians may have a still fuller and deeper knowledge of the privilege and power of their salvation 1:15-18.

II. The threefold manifestation of God's power. Chs. 1:19 to 2:22.

1. God's power was manifested in relation to Christ (1:19-23) in three ways:

(a) Resurrection.

(b) Ascension.

(c) Exaltation.

2. His power was manifested in relation to the individual in the following three ways:

(a) Spiritual resurrection. 2:1-5.

(b) Spiritual ascension. v. 6.

(c) Power to do good works and show forth God's grace throughout eternity. vv. 7-10.

3. His power was manifested in relation to the whole of humanity (2:11-22). It involved three classes:

(a) The Gentiles (vv. 11-13). In relation to Israel, they were foreigners; in relation to the covenants, they were strangers, for all the covenants were made with Israel; in relation to God they were condemned. But now they are made nigh by the blood of Christ.

(b) The Jews (vv. 14-17). Between Jew and Gentile there existed a rigid line of demarcation in regard to religion. In the temple at Jerusalem, there was a special court for the Gentiles, separated from the "court of Israel" by a wall (the middle wall of partition, verse 14), this wall bearing notices to the effect that Gentiles were forbidden to proceed farther under penalty of death. But in the spiritual temple of God there is no longer a dividing line; Jew and Gentile have "access by one Spirit unto the Father."

(c) The Church of God (vv. 19-22). The Gentile worshipped in his idol temple, the Jew in the great sanctuary at Jerusalem. Now, both have left these buildings made with hands, to form one great spiritual temple, whose chief cornerstone is Christ, whose foundation, the apostles and New Testament prophets, and whose stones are individual Christians—the whole forming a great temple inhabited by God through the Spirit.

III. A threefold statement concerning Paul. Ch. 3.

1. Paul's ministry—to preach the mystery of the Gospel. The mystery was the great truth that Jew and Gentile should be fellow-heirs and members of the same body (v. 6). It was hid in God from the foundation of the world, and not revealed under the Old Testament dispensation (vv. 5, 9). The Old Testament Scriptures taught the salvation of the Gentiles, but not their forming one body with the Jews.

2. Paul's prayer. vv. 13-19.

3. Paul's praise. vv. 20, 21.

PRACTICAL SECTION: THE CHURCH'S WALK. CHS. 4-6.

I. A threefold exhortation to the whole church. Chs. 4:1 to 5:21.

1. An exhortation to unity (4:1-16). Notice three facts concerning unity:

(a) Qualities essential to unity; lowliness and meekness, long-suffering, forbearance. vv. 1-3.

(b) A description of the unity. vv. 4-6.

(c) The method of producing unity: by the use of the gifts, and by the ministry, whose office is to bring the body into spiritual perfection and oneness with Christ. vv. 7-16.

2. An exhortation to live a new life—to put off the old man and not live like other Gentiles; to put on the new man and live in conformity to God's plan. 4:17-32.

3. An exhortation to a new walk (5:1-20). Dr. Riley suggests three features of the believer's walk as suggested by the threefold mention of the word "walk."

(a) Walk in love. vv. 1-7.

(b) Walk in the light. vv. 8-14.

(c) Walk circumspectly. vv. 15-20.

II. A threefold exhortation to the family. Chs. 5:21 to 6:9.

    1. Wives and husbands. 5:21-33.

    2. Children and parents. 6:1-4.

    3. Slaves and masters. 6:5-9.

III. A threefold expression of spiritual life. Ch. 6:10-24.

    1. Power (6:10-17). An exhortation to put on the whole armor of God (this figure was probably suggested by the armor of the Roman soldiers who were guarding Paul) that the Christian may realize His strength and fight His battles.

    2. Prayer (6:18-19). The "when," "how," and "for whom" of prayer.

    3. Peace (6:20-24). After a personal reference to Tychicus the apostle closes with a benediction.

CHAPTER IV

PHILIPPIANS

Theme. The epistle to the Philippians has been called "the sweetest of all of Paul's writings," and "the most beautiful of all of Paul's letters, in which he bares his very heart and every sentence glows with a love more tender than woman's." Throughout the epistle there breathes forth a spirit of love on the part of Paul for the Philippians; and their attitude toward him shows that his love was mutual. There are no controversial matters discussed, no severe rebukes, no aching heart on the part of Paul because of any serious disorders. There were some divisions, it is true, but they did not seem to be of any serious nature. In dealing with them the apostle uses rare tact and judgment. Instead of hurling severe denunciations against the parties involved, he creates an atmosphere of unity and love by the frequent use of words suggesting fellowship and co-operation—such words as "yoke fellow," "fellow soldier," and like words suggesting the thought of unity and fellowship. He creates an atmosphere of faith and worship by the repeated use of the name of the Lord, and makes them forget their petty differences as he paints for them a wonderful pen-picture of the One, who, though He was in the form of God, emptied Himself and humbled Himself for the salvation of others. In seeking for the theme we shall be guided by the frequent use of certain words. A great scholar said the sum of Philippians is "I rejoice, rejoice ye." The letter is full of joy. In every chapter, like the tinkle of silvery bells sound forth the words "joy," "rejoice," "rejoicing." In spite of imprisonment and in spite of the fact that he is resting in the shadow of the executioner's block, the apostle can rejoice. We shall sum up the theme as follows: the joy of Christian life and service, manifested under all circumstances.

Occasion for Writing. Epaphroditus, the messenger of the Philippian church, and the one entrusted with a gift to the apostle, fell sick on his arrival at Rome. On his recovery he returned to Philippi and Paul took advantage of this circumstance to send a letter of thanks and exhortation to the church about whose condition Epaphroditus had notified Paul.

When Written. About 64 A. D. during Paul's first imprisonment at Rome.

Contents

I. Paul's Situation and Labors at Rome.   Ch. 1.

1. Paul's salutation (1:1-11).
2. His joyfulness in prison (vv. 12-30).

(a) His joyfulness in spite of bonds (vv. 12-14). His imprisonment has turned out to the furtherance of the Gospel. The news of his imprisonment and preaching has been spread all over the military quarters and from thence to other parts of the city. The Christians at Rome have been inspired to evangelistic effort by his boldness.

(b) His joyfulness in spite of those who, in the spirit of party are preaching the gospel from insincere motives (probably the Judaizers) (15-18). But since Christ is being proclaimed, the apostle will rejoice.

(c) His joyfulness in spite of the prospect of death (vv. 19-30). It matters little to the apostle whether he lives or dies, for in either case his desire is to glorify Christ. It would be better for him to die and be with Christ; yet he would rather live and finish his work, and further the faith of the Philippians. He has hopes that he will be released and so be able to visit them. But whether he sees them or not, he desires that they walk worthy of the Gospel, proclaiming its message in spite of persecution.

II. Three Examples of Self-denial. Ch. 2.

Paul begins with an exhortation to unity, which was in danger of being marred by some minor differences among the believers (vv. 1-2). This unity was to be effected on their part by the spirit of humility and self-denial (vv. 3, 4). "Look not every man on his own things, but every man also on the things of others." The apostle then mentions three examples of those whose principle of life was sacrifice for others.

1. The example of Christ (2:5-16), who, though He was on equality with God, emptied Himself of His glory, stripped Himself of His power and humbled Himself even to the death of the cross—for others.

The apostle then adds a threefold exhortation:

(a) An exhortation to perseverance in the faith (vv. 12, 13).

(b) An exhortation to obedience (vv. 14-16).

(c) An exhortation to missionary activity (v. 16).

2. The example of Timothy (2:17-24). He was a minister who fully exemplified Paul's exhortation in verse 4. Compare vv. 20, 21.

3. The example of Epaphroditus (2:25-30). In this Christian, we have an example of one who freely poured out his life for others. Having been brought nigh unto death through overwork, he was troubled, not because of his own affliction but

because the news of his sickness had caused sorrow to others.

III. Warnings Against Error. Ch. 3.

1. A warning against legalism (3:1-14). To one not acquainted with these teachers it would seem unduly severe to refer to them as "dogs" and "evil-workers," but Paul saw in their teaching of salvation by the externals of the law something that would undermine Christian life and faith. Accordingly he denounces the Judaizers as enemies of the gospel. Paul had as much to boast of in the way of social and religious privileges as these Judaizing teachers (vv. 4-6), but he has rejected them all and counts them but as refuse (vv. 7, 8) that he may win Christ and be found in Him having the righteousness, not of the law, but of faith (vv. 9, 10). His justification and sanctification by faith in Christ has not lulled him into a careless security, for he still presses toward the goal of that perfection which will be consummated at the first resurrection (vv. 11-14).

2. An exhortation to unity in doctrine (vv. 15, 16). Those who are spiritually mature are to take this same attitude toward Christian perfection mentioned by Paul, and to agree on it. If there are minor differences, in non-essentials, God will make even these clear. These verses reveal the subject that was causing divisions among the Philippians; namely, the subject of Christian perfection.

3. A warning against Antinomianism (lawlessness) (vv. 17-19). From the Jewish side the church was exposed to the danger of legalism. From the Gentile side, to the danger of antinomianism, a doctrine which taught that the believer was under no law whatsoever. Adherence to this teaching often resulted in shipwreck of faith and purity.

4. An exhortation to holiness (vv. 20, 21). They

are to maintain a heavenly walk, for they have a heavenly hope—a hope of glorification at the coming of the Lord.

IV. Concluding Exhortations. Ch. 4.

    1. Exhortations to:
    (a) Steadfastness. v. 1.
    (b) Like-mindedness. v. 2.
    (c) Co-operation with Christian workers. v. 3.
    (d) Rejoicing. v. 4.
    (e) Forbearance and gentleness. v. 5.
    (f) Freedom from anxiety vv. 6, 7.
    (g) Holy-mindedness. v. 8.
    (h) Practical Christianity. v. 9.
    2. Thanks to the believers for their gifts. vv. 10-20.

    3. Salutations and benedictions. vv. 21-23.

COLOSSIANS

Theme. The occasion for the writing of the epistle to the Colossians was the introduction of erroneous teaching in the church. It seems that there had appeared in their midst a teacher who was propagating a doctrinal system that was a mixture of Jewish legalism and pagan philosophy. It was the pagan element in the system—after Paul's time known as Gnosticism—that constituted the greatest danger to the faith of the church. The Gnostics prided themselves on their possession of a wisdom far deeper than that revealed in the sacred Scriptures, a wisdom which was the property of a favored few. ("Gnostic" comes from a Greek word meaning "knowledge.") They believed that matter was inherently evil, therefore a holy God could not have created it. Angels, claimed they, were the creators of matter. A pure God did not have direct communication with sinful man, but communicated with him through a chain of intermediary angels who formed, as it were, a ladder from earth to heaven.

Dr. Jowett thus describes one form of their belief: "Flesh is essentially evil, God is essentially holy; between the essentially evil and the essentially holy there can be no communion. It is impossible, says the heresy, for the essentially holy to touch the essentially evil. There is an infinite gulf between the two and the one cannot touch and be intimate with the other. The heresy then had to devise some means whereby this gulf could be crossed, and by which the essentially holy God could come into communion with the essentially evil state in which mankind was dwelling. What could it do? It said that out of the essentially holy God there emanated a being slightly less holy, and then out of the second holy one there emanated a third one less holy still and out of the third, a fourth, and so on, with increasing dilution of holiness, with divinity more and more impoverished, until one appeared (Jesus), who was so emptied of divinity, holiness, so nearly like man, that he could touch man." It will be clearly seen that this heresy dealt a blow at the sovereignty, deity and mediatorship of Jesus, and placed Him in the same class as mediating angels. Paul meets this error by showing that Jesus, instead of being a mere intermediary angel, is the Creator of the universe, the Creator of the angels themselves. He exalts the Lord Jesus to His God-appointed place as Head of the universe, and the one mediator reconciling the entire creation to God. We shall sum up the theme as follows: The pre-eminence of Christ: He is first in nature, first in the church, first in resurrection, ascension and glorification; He is the only mediator, Saviour and source of life.

Occasion for Writing. The Colossians, having heard of Paul's imprisonment, sent Epaphras, their minister, to inform the apostle concerning their state. (1:7, 8). From Epaphras Paul learned that false teachers were trying to supplement the Christian faith by a doctrine which was a mixture of Judaism and heathen philosophy. To combat this error he wrote the epistle.

When Written. Colossians, being sent by the same messenger who bore Ephesians and Philemon —Tychicus—was probably written about the same time.

Note. Colossians was a city of Phrygia, a province of Asia Minor.

Contents

I. Introduction: Greetings. 1:1-12.

II. Explanation: True Doctrine Declared. 1:13 to 2:3.

III. Refutation: False Doctrine Exposed. 2:4-23.

IV. Exhortation: Holy Conduct Required. 3:1 to 4:6.

V. Conclusion: Salutations. 4:7-18.

I. Introduction: Greetings. 1:1-12.

1. Paul's greeting. 1:1, 2.

2. His thanksgiving (1:3-8). He thanks God for the love and fruitfulness of the Colossian church, which was made known to him by Epaphras, the minister, and the probable founder of the church.

3. His prayer. 1:9-12.

II. Explanation: True Doctrine Declared. 1:13 to 2:3.

1. The person and position of Christ. 1:14-19.

(a) He is our Redeemer because of His atoning blood. vv. 13, 14.

(b) He is the head of the natural creation—the universe—for He is its Creator. vv. 15-17.

(c) He is the head of the spiritual creation—the Church—because as the resurrected One He brought it into being. v. 18.

(d) He is the pre-eminent One, for in Him dwells the fulness of the divine powers and attributes. v. 19.

2. The work of Christ—a work of reconciliation. 1:20 to 2:3.

(a) The full extent of the reconciliation—the entire universe, material as well as spiritual. v. 20.

(b) The subjects of the reconciliation—those who were once enemies of God. v. 21.

(c) The purpose of the reconciliation—that men may be presented holy, flawless and irreproachable in the sight of God. v. 22.

(d) The condition for the full consummation of the reconciliation—a continuance in the faith. v. 23.

(e) The minister of the message of reconciliation —Paul (1:24 to 2:3). By his sufferings he is filling up the measure of Christ's sufferings. (In a sense, Christ still suffers through the persecuted members of His church. See Acts 9:4.) His ministry is to reveal the great mystery of the ages; namely, that Christ is in them, the hope of glory. This explains his interest for the Colossians though he has never seen them (2:1-3).

III. Refutation: False Doctrine Exposed. 2:4-23.

Paul warns the Colossians not to be led astray by the false reasonings of philosophers (2:4-7), for in Christ they have the fullness of divine revelation (2:3). He warns against the following errors:

1. Gnosticism (vv. 8-10). The believers are to beware of being entrapped by the arguments of human philosophy, which is simply the "A-B-C" (rudiments) of worldly knowledge (v. 8). They have no need of further perfection of the so-called higher knowledge of the Gnostics, for as Christians they are filled with the fullness of Him in whom dwells all the fullness of the Godhead in bodily form, and who is the head of all angelic powers.

2. Legalism (vv. 11-17). In these verses Paul shows:

(a) The believer's relation to the rite of circumcision (vv. 11, 12). They have undergone a spiritual circumcision, which represents a death to the sins of

the body, which death is outwardly expressed by the
Christian ordinance of baptism.

(b) Their relation to the moral law (vv. 13-15).
Dead in trespasses and sins, they were condemned
by the Law, but Christ, by His death, paid the penalty
of the Law and cancelled the debt against them.
(Compare Gal. 3:13, 14.)

(c) Their relation to the ceremonial law (vv. 15,
16). The feasts, holy days and other Jewish ceremonial observances were but types and shadows point-
ing forward to Christ. Now since Christ has come
and fulfilled the types, the latter are unnecessary.
Therefore the Christian is not bound to observe any
Jewish holy days or feasts.

3. A false mysticism (vv. 18, 19). Mysticism is
the teaching that, by direct communion with God, a
deeper knowledge of divine truths may be acquired,
than that afforded by the Scriptures. The Colossians
are not to be deceived by those who teach that angels
are to be worshiped, and who base their doctrine upon
fancied revelations from the other world.

4. Asceticism (vv. 20-23). By asceticism we
mean that doctrine which teaches that mortification of
body and the renunciation of physical comforts are
necessary to holiness. Those prohibitions against
tasting certain foods and enjoying physical comforts
are simply man-made rules for the attainment of holiness (vv. 21, 22). These restrictions though lending
a show of humility and piety to those practicing them,
cannot in themselves mortify the deeds of the flesh
(v. 23). The Christian does not need these prohibitions, for he has died to sin and is living a new life
with Christ (v. 20).

IV. Exhortation: Holy Conduct Required. 3:1 to
4:6.

1. The believer's union with Christ, and his conduct in view of this fact. 3:1-4.

2. Death to the "old man"—the putting off of lusts of the lower nature. vv. 5-9.

3. The putting on of the "new man"—the cultivating of the graces and virtues of the new life in Christ. vv. 10-17.

4. Admonitions to the family. 3:18 to 4:1.

5. Concluding exhortations. 4:2-6.

V. Conclusion: Salutations. Ch. 4:7-18.

1. The mission of Tychicus and Onesimus. vv. 7-9.

2. Salutations from different individuals. vv. 10-14.

3. Salutations from Paul. vv. 15-17.

4. Benediction. v. 18.

CHAPTER V

FIRST THESSALONIANS

(Read through the entire Epistle, comparing Acts 17:1-9)

Theme. The first reading of this epistle will reveal the fact that there is one theme that stands out above all others—the second coming of the Lord. It will be noticed that each chapter ends with a reference to that event. Paul deals with this truth more in its practical than doctrinal aspect, applying it directly to the attitude and life of the believer. So we may sum up the theme of this epistle as follows: The coming of the Lord in relation to the believer's encouragement, comfort, watchfulness, and sanctification.

Why Written. The epistle was written for the following purposes:

1. To comfort the believers during persecution. 3:1-5.

2. To comfort them concerning some of their dead who had died in the faith (4:13). The Thessalonians feared that the departed ones would lose the joy of witnessing the Lord's return.

3. It seemed that some, in expectation of the Lord's soon coming had fallen into the error of supposing that it was not necessary to work. 4:11, 12.

When Written. Written from Corinth shortly after Paul's departure from Thessalonica.

Contents. Mr. Robert Lee, of London, gives the following helpful outline:

The coming of the Lord is—

I. An **inspiring** hope for the young convert. Chap. 1.

43

II. An **encouraging** hope for the faithful servant. Chap. 2.

III. A **purifying** hope for the believer. 3:1 to 4:12.

IV. A **comforting** hope for the bereaved. 4: 13-18.

V. A **rousing** hope for the sleepy Christian. Chap. 5.

Paul with true humility and Christian courtesy mentions his co-workers, placing them on a level with himself (1:1). For what three things did Paul commend the believers (v. 3, compare 1 Cor. 13:13 and contrast the first words of Rev. 2:2)? How did Paul preach the Gospel to these believers (v. 5)? Of whom did they become followers (v. 6, compare 1 Cor. 11:1)? How did they receive the gospel (v. 6, compare Acts 13:50-52)? What was their relation to the other churches (v. 7)? What was their relation to the evangelization of the surrounding country (v. 8)? What attitude on their part in relation to sin and to God secured their salvation (v. 9)? What was their present attitude (v. 10)?

To what event does Paul have reference in 2:2? Acts 16:19-40. What is said concerning his motives in preaching the Gospel (vv. 3-6)? What is said concerning his attitude toward these believers (vv. 7-12)? Could Paul, as an apostle, have claimed financial support? 1 Cor. 9:6, 14. Why did he not require it from the Thessalonians (2:6, 9)? What testimony should every true minister of the Gospel have (v. 10)? How did the Thessalonians receive the Gospel (v. 13)? With whom does Paul compare them (v. 14)? What did he say was the culminating sin of the Jewish nation (v. 16, compare Matt. 23:13)? What was Paul's desire when he was at Athens (v. 18, compare Acts 17:15)? What will be a source of rejoicing of the minister of the Gospel in heaven (v. 19)?

Who joined Paul at Athens (3:1, 2, compare Acts 17:15)? Why did Paul send Timothy from there to the Thessalonians (3:2, 3)? What had Paul told them to expect (v. 4, compare Acts 14:22)? What did he fear (v. 5)? What news did Timothy bring back (v. 6)? What was very life to the apostle (v. 8)? What was his earnest desire (v. 10)? His prayer (vv. 11, 12)? Was that in verse 12 an important prayer (John 13:34, 35; Rom. 13:9; 1 Cor. 13:13; Gal. 5:6)? What would be the consummation of their love (v. 13)?

Against what sin common among the Gentiles, does Paul warn them (4:1-7)? What does Paul say concerning his authority (v. 8)? By what power does he exercise his authority (v. 8, compare Acts 15:28)? What truth should a believer know naturally as a child of God (v. 9, compare 1 John 3:18)? To what command does Paul have reference in verse 11 (2 Thess. 3:10)? For what two reasons was this command given (v. 12)? Where did Paul learn the truths set forth in vv. 13-18 (v. 15)?

How will the day of the Lord come in relation to the unbeliever (5:1-3)? Will it come as a thief in the night to the believer (v. 4)? Though we may not know the exact time of the Lord's coming, may we know when it is "at the door"? Matt. 24:32. To what does Paul liken the sinful condition of the world (v. 7)? What relation has v. 9 to the teaching that the church will pass through the tribulation? What is to be the believer's attitude toward their leaders (vv. 12, 13)? What admonition is given to those who might be inclined to suppress the genuine manifestations of the Spirit (v. 19)? What admonition is given to those who would exalt manifestations above the preaching of the Word (v. 20)? What is to be our attitude toward prophesyings and messages in tongues (v. 21)? What is God's perfect plan for every believer (v. 23)? When will that work be consummated (v. 23, compare Phil. 3:21; 1 John 3:2)? What makes possible of fulfillment the prayer uttered in v. 23 (v. 24)?

SECOND THESSALONIANS

(Read the entire epistle)

Theme. Second Thessalonians sets forth the second coming of the Lord in its relation to persecuted believers, unrepentant sinners, and an apostate church.

Why Written. The epistle was written for the following purposes:

1. To comfort believers during a new outbreak of persecutions. 1:4.

2. To correct a false teaching to the effect that the day of the Lord had already come (2:1). The severe persecutions had led some to believe that the great tribulation had begun.

3. To warn some who were walking disorderly. 3:6.

When Written. The epistle was written soon after Paul's first epistle to the same church.

Contents. These center round the teaching of the second coming of the Lord in relation to—

I. Persecuted Believers. 1:1-7.

II. The Unrepentant. 1:8-12.

III. Apostasy. 2:1-12.

IV. Service. 2:13 to 3:18.

Paul begins this epistle with the usual salutation (1:1, 2). He thanks God for the fact that the believers are growing in grace and love (v. 3), and commends them for their patience in persecutions (v. 4). Their patience in these persecutions shows that they believe that God's justice will finally prevail (v. 5), when the wicked will suffer (v. 6), and the righteous will be given rest (v. 7). This will take place after that Christ has taken away His people (v. 10).

Chapter 2 is the heart of the epistle. The words "day of Christ" (v. 2) should read "day of the Lord." The words "day of the Lord" refer to that period of time during which God will deal in judgment with Israel and the nations, which period will be one of great tribulation (compare Joel 1:15; 2:1; 3:14; Isa.

2:10-22). It appears that some false teachers had been spreading the belief that the day of the Lord had already come (2:2). This teaching they bolstered up by pretended spiritual revelations, and a forged letter, supposedly from Paul (v. 2). This teaching caused great consternation among the believers, who were fearful that they had missed the rapture about which Paul had spoken in the first epistle. To correct the false belief Paul mentioned the following events that must precede the coming of the day of the Lord:

1. A falling away on the part of the professed church. v. 3.

2. The catching away of God's people (v. 7). This is not directly stated, but the implication is very strong. "He that letteth (i. e., hinders) will let, until he be taken out of the way." Here reference is made to a power that is hindering the mystery of iniquity from coming to its consummation. The direct reference is to the Holy Spirit; the indirect to the church in which the Spirit dwells. Our Lord referred to believers as the salt of the earth, i. e., the element that preserves, and that hinders corruption. Matt. 5:13. Once this preserving element is removed, iniquity and lawlessness will flood the earth.

3. The revelation of Antichrist (vv. 3, 4). What is the general teaching of the Scriptures concerning this man? Dan. 7:8, 11, 21, 25; Dan. 8:23; Dan. 9:27; John 5:43; 1 John 4:3; Rev. 13:4-8; 19:19.

Chapter 3 contains sundry exhortations that require no especial explanation.

CHAPTER VI

FIRST TIMOTHY

Theme. The first epistle to Timothy is the first of those known as the Pastoral Epistles (the others are Titus and 2 Timothy), so called because they are addressed to ministers for the purpose of instructing them in church government. The epistle we are now studying was written to Timothy, Paul's faithful companion and disciple. It was written after the apostle's release following his first imprisonment. His movements after this event cannot be traced with certainty. It is believed that he visited Spain. Rom. 15:24. He then sailed to Miletus and came to Colosse. Philemon 22. From there he went to Ephesus where he left Timothy to take charge of the church, which was imperiled by false teaching. 1 Tim. 1:3. Passing north, Paul came to Troas where he took ship for Macedonia. 1 Tim. 1:3. From Macedonia he wrote the epistle to instruct Timothy concerning his duties and also to encourage him, for the young man was of a sensitive and retiring disposition, and consequently inclined to be backward in asserting his authority. We shall sum up the theme as follows: The qualifications and duties of the Christian minister, and his relation to the church, the home and the world.

Why Written. To instruct Timothy in the duties of his office, to encourage him, and to warn him against false teachers.

When Written. Probably in Macedonia during the interval between Paul's two imprisonments.

Contents

III. Ministerial Qualifications. 3:1-13.
IV. False Doctrine. 3:14 to 4:11.
V. Pastoral Instructions. 4:12 to 6:2.
VI. Concluding Exhortations. 6:3-21.

I. Sound Doctrine. Ch. 1.

1. Salutation (1:1, 2).
2. Timothy's special work at Ephesus (vv. 3-11). He was to contend for sound doctrine. The church was menaced by the following errors:

(a) Gnosticism (v. 4). The theories and endless genealogies of Gnosticism (genealogies of celestial powers and of mediating angels) simply led to useless speculation.

(b) Legalism (vv. 5-11). The object of Paul's charge ("the end of the commandment") is to teach love springing from a pure conscience and genuine faith (v. 5). But some have swerved from the principle of love as the ruling power in the believer's life. They have been teaching justification by the law, although they have no qualifications as teachers (vv. 6-7). They are ignorant of the fact that the law was not intended for those in whose hearts it is written; but its purpose is to awaken the conscience of sinners (vv. 8-11).

3. Paul's testimony (vv. 12-17). The chief of sinners has become the chief of saints; the blasphemer has become the preacher; the destroyer of the church has become its builder. Unto him, the chiefest of sinners was mercy shown, in order that he might be a living example of God's mercy.

4. The charge to Timothy (vv. 18-20). The exhortation of verse 5 is repeated, enforced by two facts:

(a) The reminder of the prophecies that had been uttered at his ordination (v. 18; compare Acts 13:1, 2).

(b) The warning drawn from the doctrinal shipwreck of two teachers whom Paul had excommunicated (vv. 19, 20).

II. Public Prayer. Ch. 2.

1. For whom to pray. Christians are to pray for all men, especially for kings and those in authority. vv. 1-7.

2. The attitude of men and women in public prayer. vv. 8-15.

(a) The men are to pray, lifting up hands unsullied by sin, and having hearts free from secret grudges and unbelief. v. 8.

(b) Women are to dress modestly, adorning themselves with good works rather than with gaudy apparel (vv. 8-10). Women are to observe the God-appointed order of the sexes; namely, that the man is the head of woman, and the one exercising authority in the home and in the church (vv. 11-14). Generally speaking woman's sphere of activity is in the home rather than in the ministry (v. 15). Note that in order to have a well balanced interpretation of verse 12 it is necessary to bear in mind the following two facts: (1) The emphasis in verse 12 seems to be on the woman's usurping of authority over the man; i. e., taking to herself an authority that God has not given her. (2) Paul is speaking in general terms and particularly of married women. Other scriptures show plainly that God, in particular cases grants a ministry to women. Ex. 15:20, 21; Judges 4:4; 2 Kings 22:14; Joel 2:28; Acts 21:8, 9; Rom. 16:1; 1 Cor. 11:5; Phil. 4:3.

III. Ministerial Qualifications. Ch. 3:1-13.

1. Necessary qualifications for bishops (vv. 1-7). The local churches of Paul's time, instead of being ruled by one pastor, were governed by a group of elders or bishops (overseers). Acts 20:28; Titus 1:5, 6, 7; 1 Pet. 5:1-3; Phil. 1:1. This was evidently the best arrangement for those days. Later, one of the elders was appointed to a place of leadership over the others, and finally each local church came to be governed by one elder or overseer, in co-operation with

deacons. This change was perfectly permissible because the New Testament does not lay down a hard and fast system of church government. It sets forth fundamental principles and then allows every church to organize itself according to the needs of the particular age and land.

2. The necessary qualifications for deacons (vv. 8-13). The deacons were those entrusted with the temporal affairs of the church, such as the handling of funds, etc.

IV. False Doctrine. 3:14 to 4:11.

1. The purpose of Paul's instructions is now mentioned in the verses that form the key to the epistle (vv. 14, 15). It is that Timothy may know how to act in all matters pertaining to the house of God, which is the church of the living God and the repository of the truth.

2. The mystery of godliness (v. 16). The foundation of this truth of which the church is the guardian, is the mystery of godliness, which mystery comprises the following fundamentals of the Gospel:

(a) Christ's incarnation: "God was manifest in the flesh."

(b) Christ's resurrection: "justified in the Spirit." (Compare Rom. 1:4.) The world by crucifying Christ declared Him unrighteous; God, by raising Him from the dead declared Him righteous (justified Him).

(c) Christ's manifestation: "seen of angels." 1 Cor. 15:5-8.

(d) Christ's proclamation: "preached unto the Gentiles."

(e) Christ's acceptation: "believed on in the world."

(f) Christ's exaltation: "received up into glory."

3. In contrast to the mystery of **godliness,** Paul mentions the mystery of **ungodliness** (4:1-5). In the last days there will be an apostasy from the faith **(v. 1).** In Paul's days this apostasy was represented by

the Gnostic heresy. "The special error herein attacked is the Gnostic heresy; and seven features of this false doctrine are apparent in the pastoral epistles: The claim to superior knowledge, insight, illumination; a spurious religion with profitless and barren speculation; a practical lawlessness; cauterizing the conscience with a hot iron; an allegorical interpretation of Scripture, explaining away the resurrection, etc.; an empty form of godliness in which words took the place of works; a compromise between God and Mammon reducing godliness to a matter of worldly gain; a pretense of superior sanctity that licensed even flagrant sins by profession of a pure motive."

4. Timothy's attitude toward erroneus teaching (vv. 6-11). He is to avoid those religious theories and speculations that teach a fruitless asceticism. Bodily exercise (in a religious sense), such as fasting and abstaining from certain foods, has a limited temporal value; but godliness is profitable for all things both in time and in eternity (vv. 7-11).

V. Pastoral Instructions. 4:12 to 6:2.

1. Instructions relating to Timothy himself. 4:12-16.

2. Instructions relating to different classes in the church:

(a) Old and young men and old and young women (5:1, 2).

(b) Widows (vv. 3-16). It was the custom of the early church to care for destitute widows (Acts 6:1). Timothy is instructed to see to the support of those widows who are needy and who are of blameless character (vv. 3-8). Many commentators believe that another class of widows is mentioned in verses 9, 10; namely those who took service with the church as deaconesses and who pledged themselves to devote themselves to different forms of charitable service. The younger widows were to be refused for they would in many cases break their agreement with the church and marry (vv. 11-16).

(c) Elders (vv. 17-25). Those elders who governed well and who taught were to receive generous remuneration (vv. 17-18). Any accusation against them not substantiated by two or more witnesses was to be ignored (v. 19). Where it is proved that an elder has been guilty of gross sin, he is to be rebuked publicly (v. 20). Timothy is not to be hasty in ordaining elders (v. 22). To lay hands on a man is to identify himself with his sin. Timothy is to exercise caution in ordaining elders, for though the sins and failings of some men are apparent, in others they do not come immediately to light (vv. 24, 25).

(d) Slaves (6:1, 2). Slaves are to perform conscientious service to believing and unbelieving masters.

VI. Concluding Exhortations. 6:3-21.

Timothy is exhorted—

1. To separate himself from those false teachers who teach contrary to Paul's doctrine, and who suppose that religion is for purpose of material gain. vv. 3-10.

2. To flee the love of money and to follow after the true riches which consist of Christian virtues. v. 11.

3. To fight in the glorious struggle for the faith and to grasp the prize of life eternal. v. 12.

4. To keep Paul's charge to him flawless and irreproachable. vv. 13-16.

5. To charge the rich not to trust in their wealth but in God who is the Owner of all things; and to so use their money here as to bring for them interest throughout eternity. vv. 17-19.

6. To guard the sacred trust, avoiding the philosophic theories of Gnosticism. vv. 20, 21.

SECOND TIMOTHY

Theme. After Paul had left Titus at Crete, he sailed north intending to pass on to Nicopolis by the way of Troas and Macedonia. Titus 3:12. Trophimus, his traveling companion, fell sick on the voyage, and was left at Miletus. 2 Tim. 4:20. Sailing to Troas the apostle stayed in the house of one named Carpus. About that time persecution arose against the Christians, instigated by the emperor Nero, who accused them of burning Rome. Paul, the acknowledged leader of the Christians, was probably arrested at Troas, and so sudden must his arrest have been, that some of his belongings were left behind (2 Tim. 4:13). On arriving at Rome, the apostle was placed in close confinement. Knowing that his martyrdom was approaching, he wrote this, his last letter to Timothy, begging the latter to visit him. Paul was sorely in need of his son in the faith, for those in Asia who should have supported him had deserted him; because of the recent persecution, most of the Christians were afraid to befriend him. Knowing that the timidity of Timothy's disposition might cause him to shrink from the risk of persecution that a visit to the capital might entail, Paul exhorts him not to fear persecution, nor to be ashamed of him the apostle, but to be bold in his testimony and to endure hardness like a good soldier of Jesus Christ. He also advises him as to his attitude toward false teachers and their doctrines. The following theme has been suggested for the epistle: Loyalty to the Lord and the truth in view of persecution and apostasy.

Why Written. The epistle was written for the following reasons: to request Timothy's presence at Rome; to warn him against false teachers; to encourage him in his duties; to strengthen him against coming persecution.

When Written. Shortly before Paul's martyrdom at Rome.

Contents
I. Introduction. 1:1-5.

II. Exhortations in View of Coming Suffering and Persecution. 1:6 to 2:13.

III. Exhortations in View of Present Apostasy. 2:14-26.

IV. Exhortations in View of Future Apostasy. 3:1 to 4:8.

V. Conclusion. 4:9-22.

I. Introduction. 1:1-5.

The following are the contents of the introduction:

1. Paul's calling—an apostle appointed by God's will to proclaim the promise of life centered in Christ. v. 1.

2. Paul's greeting to Timothy. v. 2.

3. Paul's ceaseless prayer for him. v. 3.

4. Paul's desire to see him again, remembering Timothy's tears at their last parting. v. 4.

5. Paul's memories—the unfeigned faith of Timothy, a faith that first had its home in the heart of his mother and grandmother. v. 5.

II. Exhortations in View of Coming Suffering and Persecution. Chs. 1:6 to 2:13.

Paul exhorts Timothy—

1. To stir up—kindle into a living flame—the gift of God which was bestowed upon him at his ordination, and to put away the spirit of cowardice as inconsistent with the spirit of that gift (vv. 6, 7).

2. To be bold in the face of persecution. vv. 9-11.

3. To hold fast the trust committed to him by the power of the indwelling Spirit. vv. 13, 14.

4. To recognize the attitude that believers were taking toward the apostle:

(a) Some like those of Asia, were forsaking him. v. 15.

(b) Others like Onesiphorus were supporting him. vv. 16-18.

5. To be strong in the power of God's grace. 2:1.

6. To commit to others the instructions he had received from Paul. 2:2.

7. To be ready to face hardship—

(a) Like a soldier, yielding whole-hearted service. vv. 3, 4.

(b) Like an athlete, abiding by the rules of the game. v. 5.

(c) Like a farmer, receiving the reward of patient toil. vv. 6, 7.

8. To remember two facts:

(a) The gospel of the risen Christ which enables Paul to endure suffering for the elects' sake. vv. 8-10.

(b) The faithful saying—to suffer with Christ is to reign with Him; to deny Him is to suffer loss. vv. 11-13.

III. Exhortations in View of Present Apostasy. Ch. 2:14-26.

Timothy is exhorted:

1. To urge Christians to avoid idle discussions. 2:14.

2. To be a true teacher of the Word of God, avoiding the empty, irreverent talk of false teachers. vv. 15-21.

3. To flee, not only evil doctrine, but also evil living; to follow, not only true doctrine, but also true living. v. 22.

4. To avoid foolish and superficial speculations that cause contentions, and which hinder the work of a preacher. vv. 24-26.

IV. Exhortations in View of Future Apostasy. Chs. 3:1 to 4:8.

Timothy is exhorted:

1. To avoid false teachers, for—

(a) In the future there will arise an empty profession of religion, combining an utter lack of power with a low moral standard. 3:1-5.

(b) The ministers of this religion will be characterized by their lack of principle and opposition to the truth. vv. 6-9.

2. To abide loyally by his convictions, remembering:

(a) The lesson that suffering is the Christian's lot in this world, as illustrated by Paul's example. vv. 11-13.

(b) The lessons learned from Paul's holy life. vv. 10, 14.

(c) The lessons he has learned from the Holy Scriptures. vv. 16, 17.

3. To do his full duty as an evangelist, preaching the Word with tireless patience, adapting his teaching to every capacity, preaching, pleading, and reproving, whether the opportunities seem favorable or unfavorable (4:1, 2). He is to do this for two reasons:

(a) The people in the future, will grow impatient of sound teaching and reject it. vv. 3, 4.

(b) Paul's ministry is about to close; he is trusting Timothy to continue his work as far as he is able. vv. 5, 6.

V. Conclusion. 4:9-22.

1. An urgent request (4:9, 10). Like the message of an aged and dying father to his only son, comes Paul's request to Timothy, "Do try hard to come to me—very soon" (v. 9). The apostle is lonely. Demas has forsaken him; the others are absent on various missions; only Luke is with him.

2. Special instructions. 4:11-13.

(a) Timothy is to bring Mark, who had proved himself worthy of the apostle's confidence. v. 11.

(b) Timothy was to bring his cloak, books and parchments (v. 13). The apostle must have been in a fireless cell, and facing a cold winter. "The pathos of Paul's position is vivified by quoting from a letter of William Tyndale (an English translator of the Scriptures, who was martyred in the sixteenth century) when he was in prison for Christ's sake in the damp cells of Vivoorde, 'I entreat your Lordship,' he wrote, 'and that by the Lord Jesus, that if I must remain here for the winter, you would beg the commissary to be so kind as to send me, from the things of mine which he hath, a warmer cap. I feel the cold painfully in my head. Also a warmer cloak, for the one I have is very thin. Also some cloth to patch my leggings. My overcoat is worn out, my shirts even are worn out. He has a woolen shirt of mine if he will send it. But most of all, I entreat and implore your kindness to do your best with the commissary to be as good as to send me my Hebrew Bible, grammar and vocabulary, that I may spend my time in that pursuit.' "—Percy G. Parker.

3. A bitter opponent (vv. 14, 15). Timothy is warned against Alexander, perhaps one who had testified against Paul in court.

4. Paul's trial and first defense (vv. 16, 17). Paul's second imprisonment was more rigorous than his first. During the first imprisonment he had his own hired house; during the second, he was kept in close confinement. During the first he was surrounded by his friends; during the second, he was almost alone. In the first he was expecting a speedy release; in the second, he was looking forward to death. He was evidently arraigned on a serious charge, probably that of being one of the chief instigators of the burning of Rome. "This alteration in the treatment of Paul exactly corresponds with that which the history of the times would have led us to expect. We have concluded that his liberation took place early in A. D. 63; he was therefore far distant from Rome when the first imperial persecution of Christianity broke out, in consequence of the great fire in the following year. . . . When the alarm and indignation of the people were excited by the tremendous ruin of the conflagration which burnt down almost half of the city, it answered the purpose of Nero (who was accused of causing the fire) to avert the rage of the populace from him-

self to the already hated votaries of a new religion. Tacitus, a Roman historian, describes the success of this expedient, and relates the sufferings of the Christian martyrs, who were put to death with circumstances of the most aggravated cruelty. Some were crucified; some disguised in the robes of beasts, and hunted to death with dogs; some were wrapped with ropes impregnated with inflammable materials, and set on fire at night, that they might serve to illuminate the circus of the Vatican and the gardens of Nero, where this diabolical monster exhibited the agonies of his victims to the public, and gloated over them himself, mixing among the spectators in the costume of a charioteer. Brutalized as the Romans were by the spectacle of human combats in the amphitheater, and hardened by popular prejudice against the 'atheistical' sect, yet the tortures of the victims excited their compassion. 'A very great multitude,' as Tacitus informs us, perished in this manner; and it appears from his statement that the mere fact of professing Christianity was sufficient to justify their execution; the whole body of Christians being considered involved in the crime of firing the city. This, however, was in the first excitement which followed the fire; and even then, but few among those who perished were Roman citizens. Since that time, some years had passed, and now a decent respect would be paid to the forms of law in dealing with one, who, like Paul, possessed the privilege of citizenship. Yet we can understand that a leader of so abhorred a sect would be subjected to severe punishment.

"We have an account of the first hearing of Paul's cause from his own pen. 'When I was first heard in my defense, no man stood by me but all forsook me. I pray that it may not be laid to their charge. Nevertheless the Lord Jesus stood by me and strengthened my heart; that by me the proclamation of the Glad Tidings might be accomplished in full measure, and that all the Gentiles might hear, and I was deliv-

ered out of the lion's mouth.' We see from this statement that it was dangerous even to appear in public
as the friend or adviser of the apostle. No advocate
would venture to plead his cause, no 'Procurator' to
aid him in arranging the evidence, no 'patronus' to
appear as his supporter and to deprecate, according
to ancient usage, the sentence. But he had a more
powerful Intercessor and a wiser Advocate, who could
never leave him nor forsake him. The Lord Jesus
was always near him, but now was felt visibly present
in the hour of need. . . . From the above description
we can realize in some measure the external features of
his trial. He evidently intimates that he spoke before
a crowded audience, so that all the Gentiles might
hear; and this corresponds to the supposition, which
historically we should be led to make, that he was
tried in one of those great basilicas which stood in the
Forum. . . . The basilicas were rectangular buildings
of great size, so that a vast multitude of spectators
was always present at any trial which excited public
interest. Before such an audience it was that Paul
was called to speak in his defense. His earthly friends
had deserted him, but His heavenly Friend stood by
him. He was strengthened by the power of Christ's
Spirit and pleaded the cause not of himself only, but
of the gospel. At the same time he successfully defended himself against the first of the charges brought
against him, which perhaps accused him of conspiring
with the burners of Rome. He was delivered from the
immediate peril, and saved from the ignominious and
painful death which might have been his doom had he
been convicted on such a charge."—Conybeare and
Howson's "Life and Epistles of St. Paul."

5. Salutations and benediction. 4:19-20.

Note: Tradition tells us that Paul was beheaded
in Rome.

CHAPTER VII

TITUS

Theme. The epistle to Titus follows that of 1 Timothy in order of composition. After writing the last-named epistle, Paul sailed with Titus to Crete where he left him to set in order the unorganized churches. Titus, a heathen by birth (Gal. 2:3), was probably one of Paul's converts (Titus 1:4). He was present with the apostle at the council at Jerusalem (Acts 15), where, in spite of the insistence of the Judaizers, Paul refused to circumcise him (Gal. 2:3). The apostle had great confidence in him and entrusted him with important missions (2 Cor. 7:6, 7, 13-16; 2 Cor. 8:16-24). Knowing that the untrustworthy and vicious character of the Cretians and the presence of false teachers would render his task a difficult one, Paul wrote Titus a letter to instruct and encourage him in his duties. The epistle is short, containing only three chapters, but it compresses in a short compass a large amount of instruction embracing doctrine, morals and discipline. Martin Luther said of it: "This is a short epistle, but such a quintessence of Christian doctrine, and composed in such a manner that it contains all that is needful for Christian knowledge and life." We shall sum up the theme as follows: The organizing of a true church of Christ; and an appeal to the church to be true to Christ.

When Written. Shortly after First Timothy, probably from some point in Asia minor.

Why Written. To instruct Titus in the organization of the Cretian church and to direct him in the method of dealing with the people.

Contents

I. The Order and Doctrine of the Church. Ch. 1.

II. The Conduct of the Church. Chs. 2, 3.

I. The Order and Doctrine of the Church. Ch. 1.

1. Introductory: Paul's salutation to Titus. vv. 1-4.

2. Titus' special mission in Crete—to set in order the disorganized church. v. 5.

3. The qualifications for elders. vv. 6-9.

4. The reason for the exercising of great care in choosing elders—the presence of false teachers (vv. 10-16). Concerning these teachers notice:

(a) Their character: insubordinate and deceitful, and given to empty talk. v. 10.

(b) Their motive: material gain. v. 11.

(c) Their teaching: Jewish traditions and legends (v. 14); for example, commandments concerning the abstaining from certain foods (v. 15; compare Mark 7:1-23; Rom. 14:14).

(d) Their claims: they profess to be true teachers of the gospel, but their sinful lives belie their profession. v. 16.

Note that Paul in exposing the character of the Cretians (vv. 12, 13), quotes a Cretian poet, Epimenides (600 B. C.). Ancient writers speak of the Cretians' love of gain, ferocity, fraud, falsehood and general depravity. To "Cretianize" was proverbial for to lie, as to "Corinthianize" was for to be dissolute.

II. The Conduct of the Church. Chs. 2, 3.

1. The believer's conduct in relation to one another. 2:1-15.

2. The believer's conduct in relation to the outside world. 3:1-8.

3. What to avoid—discussions concerning celestial genealogies and minute points of the law of Moses. v. 9.

4. Whom to avoid—heretics (vv. 10, 11). A heretic is a person who causes a division in the church by teaching an unscriptural doctrine. In Paul's day,

tainted morals were often the accompaniment of tainted doctrine.

5. Concluding instructions. vv. 12-15.

PHILEMON

(Read the epistle)

Theme. The epistle to Philemon is the only example of Paul's private correspondence preserved to us. From the glimpse it affords us of the apostle's courtesy, prudence and skillful address it has been known as the "polite epistle." It does not contain any direct teaching concerning doctrine or Christian conduct. Its chief value lies in the picture it gives us of the practical outworking of Christian doctrine in everyday life, and of the relation of Christianity to social problems.

We shall gather our theme from the story told by the epistle, a story which centers around a runaway slave named Onesimus. The latter was more fortunate than some of his fellow-slaves in that he had for master a Christian, Philemon, a convert of Paul. For reasons not mentioned, Onesimus ran away from his master, and in so doing he probably took with him some of his master's property. He made his way to Rome, where he was converted under Paul's preaching. In him the apostle found a sincere convert and a devoted friend.

So dear did Onesimus become to him that Paul would have retained him to minister to him in his captivity. But the apostle had to make a sacrifice. Though Onesimus had repented of his sin, there was a call for restitution which could be made only by the slave's returning and submitting himself to his master. The claim of duty involved a sacrifice not only for Paul, but it demanded a still greater one from Onesimus, who on returning to his master would be liable to severe punishment—crucifixion was a general penalty imposed upon runaway slaves.

The sense of right required Paul to return the slave, but the constraint of love caused him to intercede for him and save him from punishment. Taking up his pen he wrote a courteous, tactful letter of eager, affectionate entreaty, identifying himself with Onesimus.

After saluting Philemon and his family (vv. 1-3), Paul commends him for his love, faith and hospitality (vv. 4-7). The apostle has a request to make. As Paul **the apostle,** he could **command;** but as Paul the **aged, the prisoner of the Lord,** he rather **beseeches** Philemon (vv. 8, 9). His request is that the latter receive again Onesimus, one who was once unprofitable, but who is now become profitable —Onesimus, Paul's own son in the faith (vv. 10-12). So attached had he become to the slave that he would have retained him as servant but without Philemon's consent he would not act (vv. 13, 14). Perhaps it was in God's providence that Onesimus should have departed for a short time, in order that he might return to be forever with his master, not as a servant but as a brother (vv. 15, 16). Paul identifies himself with Onesimus; if the latter owes anything the apostle will pay it. But Philemon should remember that to Paul he is indebted, in a sense, for his salvation (v. 19). That Philemon will obey, and even do more than Paul asks, is the latter's confidence (v. 21). The epistle concludes with the usual salutations (vv. 22-25).

From verses 16 and 21 we may safely infer that Onesimus was given his freedom. Thus by the regeneration of the individual and by the uniting of master and slave in Christ was the problem of slavery solved—at least in one family. We shall sum up the theme of the epistle as follows: the power of the gospel in the solution of social problems.

When Written. It was sent by Tychicus with the letters to the Colossians and the Ephesians.

Contents

    I. Introduction: Greetings. vv. 1-3.
   II. Commendation of Philemon. vv.4-7.
   III. Intercession for Onesimus. vv. 8-21.
   IV. Conclusion: Salutations. vv. 22-25.

The Value of the Epistle

1. Its personal value lies in the insight it gives into the character of Paul, revealing his love, humility, courtesy, unselfishness and tact.

2. Its providential value. We learn here that God may be in the most untoward circumstances (v. 15).

3. Its practical value. We are encouraged to seek and redeem the lowest and most degraded. Onesimus had nothing to commend him, for he was a runaway slave, and worse still, a Phrygian slave, from a region noted for the vice and stupidity of its inhabitants. But Paul won him for Christ.

4. Its social value. The epistle presents the relation of Christianity to slavery. During Paul's time there were about six million slaves in the Roman empire. Their lot, in general, was miserable. Considered as the property of their masters, they were completely at his mercy. They had no rights by law. For the slightest offenses they could be scourged, mutilated, crucified, or thrown to the wild beasts. No permanent marriages were allowed among them, but only temporary unions, which could be broken at the will of the masters. It may be asked, Why did not Christianity attempt to overthrow this system? Because to have done so would have required a tremendous revolution—and the religion of Christ reforms by love and not by force. It teaches principles that undermine and overthrow wrong systems. This method of reformation is well illustrated in the case of Philemon and Onesimus. **Master and slave were united in**

the Spirit of Christ, and in that union all social distinctions were obliterated. Gal. 3:28. Though Paul did not give a direct command to Philemon that he free Onesimus, the words in verses 16 and 21 would imply that such was the apostle's desire.

5. Its spiritual value. It furnishes us some striking types of our salvation. The following incidents will suggest types to the thoughtful student: Onesimus' forsaking his master; Paul's finding of him; Paul's interceding for him; his identifying himself with the slave; his offering to pay his debt; Philemon's receiving Onesimus on Paul's account; the slave's restoration to his master's favor.

CHAPTER VIII

HEBREWS

Theme. The epistle to the Hebrews was written, as its name suggests, particularly to the Jewish believers, although it has a permanent value and an abiding appeal for all believers in all ages. The reading of the epistle will reveal the fact that the body of Hebrew Christians addressed were in danger of falling away from the faith. Compared to the nation as a whole they were an obscure little company, regarded as traitors by their fellow countrymen, and the objects of their suspicion and hatred. They felt their loneliness, cut off as they were from the nation. Persecution was looming large before them. Oppressed by present trials and by the thought of future adversity, they had yielded to discouragement. They were lagging behind in spiritual progress (5:11-14); many were neglecting attendance at worship (10:24, 25). Many, wearied of the walk of faith, were looking toward the magnificent temple at Jerusalem with its sacrifices and imposing ritual. The temptation was to forsake Christianity and to turn to Judaism. To check this apostasy, this epistle was written, the chief purpose of which is to show the relation of the Mosaic system to Christianity, and the former's symbolical and transitory character. The writer first of all sets forth the superiority of Jesus Christ over all Old Testament mediators; then points out the superiority of the New Covenant to the Old, as a superiority of substance to shadow, of antitype to type, of reality to symbol. These believers were perplexed and disheartened by manifold temptations and, by the fact of their having to walk in the midst of adversity by faith in the naked word of God, without any visible support or comfort.

67

The writer of the epistle proves to them that the worthies of the Old Testament passed through similar experiences, walking by faith, trusting in the word of God in spite of all adverse circumstances and even in the face of death (Ch. 11). Therefore, like their forefathers, the believers were to "endure as seeing him who is invisible." The theme may be summed up as follows: the religion of Jesus Christ is superior to Judaism for it has a better covenant, a better high priest, a better sacrifice and a better tabernacle.

Authorship. There is no book of the New Testament whose authorship is so disputed nor any of which the inspiration is more indisputable. The book itself is anonymous. Because of difference in style from the other writings of Paul, many orthodox scholars have denied that he himself wrote it. Tertullian in the third century declared that Barnabas was the author. Luther suggested that Apollos wrote it. "Finally we may observe, that, notwithstanding the doubts which we have recorded, we need not scruple to speak of this portion of Scripture as 'the Epistle of Paul the Apostle to the Hebrews.' . . . Whether written by Barnabas, by Luke, by Clement, or by Apollos, it represented the views, and was impregnated by the influence of the great apostle, whose disciples even the chief of these apostolic men might well be called. By their writings, no less than by his own, he being dead, yet spoke."—Conybeare and Howson's "Life and Epistles of St. Paul."

Why Written. To check the apostasy of Jewish Christians who were tempted to return to Judaism.

Where Written. Evidently from Italy. 13:24.

Contents

I. The Superiority of Jesus to Old Testament Mediators and Leaders. Ch. 1:1 to 8:6.

II. The Superiority of the New Covenant to the Old. Chs. 8:7 to 10:18.

III. Exhortations and Warnings. Chs. 10:19 to 13:25.

I. The Superiority of Jesus to Old Testament Mediators and Leaders. Chs. 1:1 to 8:6.

1. Jesus is superior to the prophets because—

(a) In times past God's revelations to the prophets were partial, and given at different times and in different manners. v. 1.

(b) But in this dispensation God has given a perfect revelation through His Son. vv. 2, 3.

2. Jesus is superior to the angels, (1:4-14) for the following reasons:

(a) No individual angel was ever addressed as Son. v. 5.

(b) The Son is the object of the angel's worship. v. 6.

(c) While the angels serve, the Son reigns. vv. 7-9.

(d) The Son is not a creature, but the Creator. vv. 10-12.

(e) No angel is promised universal authority, for their function is service. vv. 13, 14.

3. Exhortation in view of the foregoing statements (2:1-4). If disobedience to the word of angels brought punishment, what will be the loss if the salvation declared by the Lord Himself be unheeded?

4. Jesus was exalted above the angels. Why was He made lower than they (2:5-18)? For the following reasons:

(a) In order that human nature might be glorified and that man might take his God-given place as ruler of the world to come. vv. 5-8.

(b) That He might fulfill God's plan in dying for all men. v. 9.

(c) That the Saviour and saved might be one. vv. 11-15.

(d) That he might fulfill all the conditions of a faithful priest. 2:16-18.

5. Jesus is greater than Moses (3:1-6), because—

(a) Moses was only part of God's household; Jesus was the Founder of the same. vv. 2, 3.

(b) Moses was only a servant; Jesus was a Son. vv. 5, 6.

6. Exhortation in view of the statements in Ch. 3:1-6 (3:7 to 4:5). The Christian is a member of a spiritual household presided over by the Son of God. But let him beware, for this privilege may be lost, just as the privilege of entering Canaan was lost by many Israelites through their faithlessness and disobedience. Though these Israelites had experienced Jehovah's salvation at the Red Sea, they did not enter the Promised Land. The sin that excluded them was the sin of unbelief—a sin, that if persisted in, will exclude the Jewish Christian from the privileges of his inheritance.

7. Jesus is greater than Joshua. 4:6-13.

(a) Joshua led the Israelites into the Rest of Canaan, which was but a type of spiritual rest into which Jesus leads the believers. vv. 6-10.

(b) Exhortation in view of this statement (vv. 11-13). "Let us, then, earnestly strive to enter that Rest of God, lest any of us should, through following the example of the disobedience of ancient Israel, miss the second opportunity. For God's word on which I base my argument, is not a thing of the past nor something external to us: it is still living; it is instinct with energy; it is keener than any two-edged sword: that can but pierce flesh, but this finds its way to the dividing line between the animal life and the immortal spirit: it pierces the deepest recesses of our nature; it analyzes the very emotions and purposes of the inmost heart. Yet there is no created thing that can escape His notice; but all things lie bare and defenseless before the eyes of Him with whom we have to reckon."—Dr. Way's translation.

8. Jesus' high priesthood. 4:14 to 5:10.

(a) The fact of Jesus' priesthood (v. 14). The believers are to cling to the faith they possess, for they are not without a faithful priest, as their non-Christian brethren might lead them to believe. Their high priest though invisible, ever intercedes for them.

(b) Jesus' qualifications as a priest:

(1) He can sympathize with human infirmity (4:14 to 5:1-3, 7-9), for He Himself, like men, has suffered temptation, and borne suffering, but with this difference—He did not sin.

(2) He was called of God, as Aaron was. 5:4-6, 10.

9. The writer breaks the thread of his thought in order to utter words of rebuke, exhortation, warning and encouragement:

(a) A rebuke (5:11-14). He is about to discuss a deep typical subject—concerning Melchizedek —but he fears that their spiritual immaturity will make it difficult for him to explain it.

(b) An exhortation (6:1-3). They are to pass the elementary state of Christian doctrine and press on to matured knowledge. The expression "principles of the doctrine of Christ" may have reference to the fundamental doctrines of Christianity in which converts were instructed before baptism.

(c) A warning (6:6-8). The warning contained in these verses is against apostasy, which is a willful rejection of the truths of the Gospel on the part of those who have experienced its power. The true nature of the sin referred to in these verses will be better understood when we remember who are being addressed and the peculiar relation of the Jewish nation to Christ. The Jews of the writer's time could be divided into two classes in relation to their attitude toward Christ: those who accepted Him for whom He claimed to be—the Son of God; and those who rejected Him as an impostor and a blasphemer. The Jewish Christian who fell away from Christianity and returned to Judaism, would by this act testify that he believed that Christ was not the Son of God but a false prophet who merited crucifixion; he would be taking sides with those who were responsible for His death. Before his conversion, this same Jewish Christian in a sense, shared the guilt of his nation in crucifying Christ; in forsaking Christ and returning to Judaism he would be rejecting the Son of God **a second time** and crucifying Him afresh (v. 6).

(d) An encouragement (vv. 9-20). Though he thus warns them the writer is confident that the believers will not fall away from the faith (v. 9). They have been earnest in the performance of good works (v. 10); he desires that they display the same earnestness in the attainment of the hope of their spiritual inheritance (v. 11). In this they are to be followers of those, who through faith and patience attained to the realization of their hope—for example, Abraham (vv. 12, 13). The Christian's hope is a sure one; it is an anchor of the soul, holding him fast in a heavenly harbor (vv. 19, 20). It is a sure hope, for it is founded on two unchangeable things: God's promise and God's oath (vv. 13-18).

10. Christ's priesthood (typified by that of Melchizedek) is superior to the Aaronic. 7:1 to 8:6.

Melchizedek is mentioned in this connection as a type of Christ. The writer uses a Jewish mode of illustration. He takes a scriptural fact as it stands and shows its typical value. Melchizedek is a type of Christ in the following respects:

(a) By reason of the meaning of his name, "King of righteousness," "King of peace." v. 2.

(b) His priesthood was not hereditary; Jewish priests were required to produce their genealogy before being admitted to office. Ezra 2:61-63. Though Melchizedek was a priest there is no record of his genealogy, and this is what is meant by the expression, "without father, without mother" (v. 3). In this respect he is a type of Christ who did not have a priestly genealogy. Heb. 7:14.

(c) The fact that there is no record either of his birth or his death is typical of the eternal nature of Christ's priesthood. This is what is meant by the expression, "having neither beginning of days nor end of life." v. 3.

11. The priesthood of Christ, typified by that of Melchizedek, is greater than that of Aaron, as shown by the following facts:

(a) In a manner of speaking, Levi, while yet in Abraham's loins, paid tithes to Melchizedek. 7:4-10.

(b) Spiritual maturity was not attainable through the Aaronic priesthood and the covenant of which it was the mediator. This is witnessed by the fact that another order of priesthood was to arise—the Melchizedek order. This change of priesthood implies a change of law. The change was effected because of the inability of the Mosaic law to bring spiritual maturity. (Compare Rom. 8:1-4.)

(c) Unlike the Aaronic priesthood, the Melchizedek priesthood was instituted with an oath (vv. 20-22). God's oath, accompanying any statement is a sign of immutability.

(d) The ministry of the priests of the Aaronic order was ended by death; but Christ has an eternal and unchangeable priesthood, for He lives forever. vv. 23-25.

(e) The Aaronic priests offered sacrifices every day; Christ offered one eternally efficacious sacrifice. 7:26-28.

(f) The Aaronic priests served in the tabernacle which was but an earthly type of the tabernacle in which Christ ministers. 8:1-5.

(g) Christ is the mediator of a better covenant. 8:6.

II. The Superiority of the New Covenant to the Old. Chs. 8:7 to 10:18.

This superiority is manifested in the following ways:

1. The Old Covenant was only temporary (8: 7-13). This fact is witnessed by the Old Testament Scriptures which teach that God will make a new covenant with His people.

2. The ordinances and sanctuary of the Old Covenant were simply types and shadows that did not bring perfect fellowship with God. 9:1-10.

3. But Christ, the true priest of the heavenly sanctuary, by one perfect sacrifice—His own Person —brought eternal redemption and perfect fellowship with God. vv. 11-15.

4. The New Covenant was sealed with better blood than that of calves and goats—the blood of Jesus. vv. 16-24.

5. The one sacrifice of the New Covenant is better than the many sacrifices of the Old. 9:25 to 10:18.

III. Exhortations and Warnings. Chs. 10:19 to 13:25.

1. An exhortation to faithfulness and steadfastness in view of the fact that they have sure access to God through a faithful high priest. 10:19-25.

2. A warning against apostasy (vv. 26-31; compare 6:4-8). Let not those who will turn away from Christ as the sacrifice for their sins think that they can find another in Judaism. To willfully and knowingly reject Him is to thrust from themselves the sacrifice that will shield them from the fiery indignation of God. One scholar suggests that, from verse 29, it may be inferred that Jewish apostates from Christianity were, before being readmitted to the synagogue, required—(1) to deny that Jesus was the Son of God, (2) to declare that His blood was rightly shed as that of a malefactor, (3) to ascribe (as the Pharisees did) the gifts of the Spirit to the operation of demons.

3. An exhortation to patience in view of the promised reward. vv. 32-36.

4. An exhortation to walk by faith (10:37 to

12:1-4). In this section it is the writer's purpose
to show that those in past ages in whom God took de-
light were those who walked by faith, and who trusted
Him in spite of all circumstances.

(a)   Faith enjoined. 10:37-39.

(b)   Faith described (11:1-3). Faith is that
which makes the believer confident that the objects
of his hope are real and not imaginary. It is manifested as shown in the case of the Old Testament
saints, by an implicit obedience to and trust in God,
in spite of appearances, and adverse circumstances.

(c)   Faith conquering through God. vv. 32-36.

(d)   Faith suffering for God. vv. 37-40.

(e)   Faith's supreme example—the Lord Jesus,
the One who gave the first impulse to our faith, and
who will bring it to its final maturity. 12:1-4.

5.   An exhortation to scrupulous obedience because of their heavenly calling (12:18-24), and because of their heavenly Leader (vv. 25-29).

6.   Concluding exhortations. 13:1-17.

(a)   To sanctified living. vv. 1-7.

(b)   To steadfast living. vv. 8, 9.

(c)   To separated living (vv. 10-16). Dr. Way's
translation will clarify verses 10-14: "Such restrictions
(v. 9, concerning clean and unclean meats) have no
application to us: we already have an altar of sacrifice of which we partake; but such as still cling to
the superseded temple service are disqualified from
partaking of it. I say so, because, when the blood
of the victims slain for the sin-offerings on the Day
of Atonement is borne into the Holy Place by the
high priests, the bodies of these victims may not, like
other sacrifices, be eaten by the worshipers, but are
burnt outside the precincts of the camp. For this reason, also, Jesus that He might consecrate God's people by His own blood, suffered without the gate, sym-
bolizing the fact that those who remain in Judaism
have no part in Him. Therefore let us, who accept
Him, go forth to Him outside the limits of Judaism,

bearing the contumely which is heaped upon Him. We shall not be homeless: an abiding city we have, but not here: we aspire to that which is yet to be."

    (d)   To submissive living. v. 17.

   7. Conclusion. vv. 18-25.

CHAPTER IX

THE GENERAL EPISTLES

The General Epistles are so called because, unlike the Pauline Epistles, they are not addressed to any particular church, but to believers in general. Two of them (Second and Third John) are addressed to particular individuals.

JAMES

Theme. The epistle of James is the practical book of the New Testament, as Proverbs is of the Old Testament. Indeed it bears a remarkable resemblance to the last-named book because of its terse, pithy statements of moral truths. It contains little direct doctrinal teaching; its chief purpose is to emphasize the practical aspect of religious truth. James was writing to a certain class of Jewish Christians in whom there was appearing a tendency to divorce faith from works. They were claiming to have faith, yet there existed among them impatience under trial, strife, respect of persons, evil speaking and worldliness. James points out that a faith which does not produce holiness of life is a dead thing, a mere assent to a doctrine, which goes no farther than the intellect. He emphasizes the need of a living, effectual faith for the attainment of Christian perfection, and goes back to the simple Sermon on the Mount in demanding real deeds of Christian life.

"There are those who talk holiness and are hypocrites; there are those who make profession of perfect love and yet cannot live peaceably with the brethren; those who are full of pious phraseology but fail in practical philanthropy. This epistle was written for them. It may not give them much comfort but it ought to give them much profit. The mysticism

that contents itself with pious frames and phrases and comes short in actual sacrifice and devoted service will find its antidote here. The antinomianism that professes great confidence in free grace, but does not recognize the necessity for corresponding purity of life, needs to ponder the practical wisdom of the epistle. The quietists who are satisfied to sit and sing themselves away to everlasting bliss ought to read this epistle until they catch its bugle note of inspiration to present activity and continuous good deeds. All who are long on theory and short on practice ought to steep themselves in the spirit of James; and since there are such people in every community and in every age, the message of the epistle will never grow old."
—D. A. Hayes.

We shall sum up the theme as follows: Practical Christianity.

Authorship. There are three persons by the name of James mentioned in the New Testament: James the brother of John (Matt. 10:2); James the son of Alphaeus (Matt. 10:3); James the brother of the Lord (Gal. 1:19). General church tradition has identified the writer of the epistle with the last-named person. This James was the head of the church at Jerusalem, and it was he who presided at the first church council. Acts 12:17; 15:13-29. The authoritative tone of the epistle well comports with the author's high position in the church. From tradition we learn some facts concerning him. Because of his holiness of life and his rigid adherence to the practical morality of the Law, he was held in repute by the Jews of his community, by whom he was surnamed "the Just" and many of whom he led to Christ. It is said that his knees were calloused like those of a camel in consequence of his constant intercession for the people. Josephus, the Jewish historian, tells us that James was stoned to death by order of the high priest.

To Whom Written. To the twelve tribes scattered abroad (1:1); i. e., to the Christian Jews of the dispersion. The whole tone of the epistle reveals the fact that it was written for Jews.

Why Written. For the following reasons:

1. To comfort Jewish Christians who were passing through severe trials.

2. To correct disorders in their assemblies.

3. To combat a tendency to divorce faith from works.

When Written. Probably about 60 A. D. It is believed to be the first epistle written to the Christian church.

Where Written. Probably at Jerusalem.

Contents

I.   Temptation as the Trial of Faith. 1:1-21.
II. Works as the Evidence of True Faith. 1:22 to 2:26.
III. Words and Their Power. 3:1-12.
IV. Wisdom, the True and the False. 3:13 to 4:17.
V.   Patience under Oppression: the Endurance of Faith. 5:1-12.
6.   Prayer. 5:13-20.

I. Temptation as the Trial of Faith. Ch. 1:1-21.

1. The purpose of temptations: to perfect Christian character (vv. 2-4). The word "temptation" is used here in its broadest sense, as including both outward persecutions and inward solicitations to evil. James shows his readers how to turn temptations into blessings by making them a source of patient endurance and so using them as the fire which tests the gold.

2. A quality to be exercised in the .successful endurance of temptation—wisdom. This wisdom is a gift from God, but is granted only on the condition of unwavering faith. vv. 5-8.

3. A source of trial and a source of temptations
—poverty and riches (vv. 9-11). The poor man is
not to be depressed because of his poverty; neither is
the rich man to be elated because of wealth. Both are
to rejoice in their high calling.

4. The reward for endurance of trial and temptation—a crown of life. v. 12.

5. The source of inward temptation to evil (vv.
13-18). Though God may send afflictions to try men,
He does not send evil impulses to tempt them. "When
a man pleads, as men often do, that 'God has made
them so;' that 'the flesh is weak;' or that 'for a mo-
ment God deserted them;' when they say that they have
done wrong because they could not do otherwise;
when they contend that each man is no better than
an automaton and that his actions are the inevitable—
and therefore the irresponsible result of conditions by
which he is surrounded—they are transferring to God
the blame of their misdoings. . . . James gives the true
sense of evil. It springs from lust—desire—which
is to each soul the harlot temptress which draws him
from the shelter of innocence, entices him, and bears
the evil offspring of committed sin."—Dear Farrar.
Far from God's sending evil impulses, it is He that
gives us that power by which we are raised to a new
and higher life (1:16-18).

6. The attitude to be shown in the view of the
foregoing facts—a control of speech and temper, a
purity of conduct and a receptive attitude toward the
Word of God. vv. 19-21.

II. Works as the Evidence of True Faith. Chs. 1:22 to 2:26.

1. True faith should be manifested in obeying as
well as hearing the Word of God. vv. 22-25.

2. True faith should be manifested in practical
religion, of which the characteristics are control of the
tongue, brotherly love, and separation from the world.
vv. 26-27.

3. True faith is shown by impartiality in dealing with the poor and the rich (2:1-13). Courtesy to the rich combined with discourtesy to the poor is a partiality that indicates weakness of faith, and which constitutes a violation of the law.

4. Faith is proved by its works (2:14-26). A superficial reading of these might indicate that James was contradicting Paul's doctrine of justification by faith. Martin Luther in his early days was strongly opposed to this epistle, since he believed that it flatly contradicted the teachings of Paul. Later in life, however, he recognized his mistake. Close study of their writings will convince us that James and Paul are in perfect agreement. Paul believes in works of godliness as well as James (See 2 Cor. 9:8; Eph. 2:10; 1 Tim. 6:17-19; Tit. 3:8). James believes in saving faith as well as Paul (See James 1:3, 4, 6; 2:5). The seeming contradiction just referred to is explained by the fact that both writers use the words "faith," "works" and "justification" with different meanings for those terms in mind. For example:

(a) The faith meant by James is the mere intellectual assent to truth that does not lead to practical righteousness—such a faith that demons have when they believe in God (2:19). "What good is it, my brethren, if a man professes to have faith, and yet his actions do not correspond? Can such faith save him?" (v. 14, Weymouth's translation.) The faith meant by Paul is an intellectual, moral and spiritual power that brings a person into vital and conscious union with God.

(b) The works meant by Paul are the dead works of legalism, done simply from a sense of duty and compulsion, and not from pure love of God. The works meant by James are the fruits of the love of God spread abroad in the heart by the Holy Spirit.

(c) The justification spoken of by Paul is the initial act by which God pronounces the sentence of acquittal on the sinner and imputes to him the righteousness of Christ. The justification spoken of by James is that continued holiness of life which proves the believer to be a true child of God.

(d) Paul has in mind the root of salvation; James the fruit. Paul is dealing with the beginning of Christian life; James, with its continuation. Paul is condemning dead works, James, dead faith. Paul overthrows the vain confidence of legalism; James, the vain confidence of the mere professor of Christianity.

III. Words and Their Power. Ch. 3:1-12.

1. A warning against the too hasty assuming of the office of teacher, in view of the great responsibility attached to that calling, and of the dangers of offending through the spoken word, which is the medium of the teacher's instruction (vv. 1, 2).

2. The power of the tongue (vv. 3-5). It is compared to a horse's bit, to a helm, and to a fire.

3. The evil of the tongue (vv. 6-12). "Yes, the tongue—that world of injustice—is a fire. It inflames the wheel of being and is ever inflamed by Gehenna. It is the sole untamable creature—a restless mischief brimmed with deadly venom. Therewith we bless the Lord and Father, and therewith we curse the human beings who have been made after His likeness. Is this inconsistency anything short of monstrous? Is it not like a fountain bubbling out of the same fissure the bitter as well as the sweet? Can a tree produce fruits not its own? Can the salt of a cursing tongue produce the sweet water of praise?"

IV. Wisdom, the True and the False. Chs. 3:13 to 4:17.

1. The manifestations of true wisdom. 3:13, 17, 18.

2. The manifestations of the false wisdom. 3:15.

V. Patience under Oppression: the Endurance of Faith. Ch. 5:1-12.

1. Concerning the oppressors and the oppressed (vv. 1-6). James is speaking of a condition which will prevail in the last days (v. 4)—that of an oppression of the laboring class on the part of the wealthy, which oppression will cease at the coming of the Lord. The judgment of the wicked rich at the destruction of Jerusalem offers a faint picture of their fate in the last days. Writes Dean Farrar: "And if these words of James were addressed to Jews and Christians about the year 61 A. D., how speedily were his warnings fulfilled, how terribly and how soon did the retributive doom fall on these wealthy and luxurious tyrants! A few years later Vespasian invaded Judea. Truly there was need to howl and weep, when, amid the horrors caused by the rapid approach of the Roman armies, the gold and silver of the wealthy oppressors were useless to buy bread, and they had to lay up, for the moth to eat, those gorgeous robes which it would have been a peril and a mockery to wear. The worshipers at the last Passover became the victims. The rich only were marked out for the worst fury of the Zealots, and their wealth sank into the flames of the burning city. Useless were their treasures in those last days, when there was heard at their door the thundering summons of the Judge! In all their rich banquets and full-fed reveling they had but fattened themselves as human offerings for the day of slaughter."

2. Concerning the Avenger (vv. 7-12). In relation to the condition described in verses 1-6 the children of God are to possess their souls in patience awaiting the coming of the Avenger and Judge, and taking Job and the prophets as examples of patient endurance.

VI. Prayer. Ch. 5:13-20.

1. Prayer in affliction. v. 13.
2. Prayer for the sick. vv. 14-16.

3. The efficacy of prayer. vv. 17, 18.

4. Our duty toward an erring brother (vv. 18-20). "So we conclude, both from the context and from the meaning of the word itself that James and Peter (1 Peter 4:8) are speaking of a restoring ministry which turns an erring brother back to the ways of the Lord, and which, through bringing him to repentance and confession of his sins, procures the forgiveness of these even though they be a 'multitude.' For it is written that 'If we confess our sins He is faithful and just to forgive us our sins and to cleanse us from all unrighteousness.' Thus, by such a ministry as that to which we are called by the last verse of James, we may not only be the means of saving a precious life for further usefulness in the world, but may be also instrumental in the putting away of sins which would otherwise confront the wrongdoer at the judgment seat of Christ."

CHAPTER X

FIRST PETER

Theme. In this epistle there is offered to us a fine illustration of how Peter fulfilled the commission given to him by the Lord—"When thou art converted strengthen thy brethren." Luke 22:32. Purified and settled through suffering, and matured by experience he was able to utter words of encouragement to bodies of Christians who were passing through fiery trials. Many of the lessons which he had learned from the Lord Himself he imparted to his readers. (Compare 1 Peter 1:10 with Matt. 13:17; 1 Peter 5:2 and John 21:15-17; 1 Peter 5:8 with Luke 22:31.) Verse 12 of the last chapter will suggest the theme of the epistle—the grace of God. Those whom he was addressing were passing through times of testing. He therefore encourages them by showing that all that was needed for strength, character and courage was provided for in the grace of God. God is the "God of all grace" (5:10) whose message to His people is, "My grace is sufficient." The theme of 1 Peter may be summed up as follows: the sufficiency of divine grace and its practical application in relation to Christian living, and to the endurance of trial and suffering.

Why Written. To encourage believers to hold fast during suffering, and to exhort them to holiness.

When Written. Probably A. D. 60.

Where Written. From Babylon. 5:13.

Contents

III. Suffering with Christ.   Ch. 4.
IV. Concluding Exhortations.   Ch. 5.

I. Rejoicing in Suffering Because of Salvation. Ch. 1:1-12.

1.   The source of our salvation   (v. 2) :
(a)   The Father who chooses.
(b)   The Spirit who sanctifies.
(c)   The Son, with whose blood we are sprinkled.
2.   The result of salvation: the new birth.   v. 3.

3.   The consummation of salvation: the acquisition of the heavenly inheritance which is reserved for the believer, while he himself is kept by the power of God. vv. 4, 5.

4. The joy of salvation (vv. 6-8). Even in the midst of trials and temptations which are but for the testing of faith, the believers can rejoice in their invisible Lord with joy unspeakable and full of glory.

5.   The mystery of salvation. vv. 9-12.

(a) The prophets who predicted the sufferings and glory of Christ, did not fully understand their own prophecies. In answer to their enquiries it was revealed to them that the salvation about which they were prophesying was not for them but for those living in another dispensation.

(b) The angels who have never sinned desire to investigate the strange joy of those who have been redeemed by Christ.

II. Suffering for Righteousness' sake. Chs. 1:13 to 3:22.

In this section we shall notice the following exhortations:

1.   To holiness (1:13-21). With alert and sober minds, the believers are to separate themselves from their former habits of life, living a life of holiness and watching for the Lord's return.

2.   To intense and sincere love of the brethren (1:22-25). This love should follow as the natural re-

sult of the purification of the soul by the Holy Spirit;
and of the new birth.

3. To spiritual growth (2:1, 2). As the new
born babe instinctively desires to feed on milk, so the
regenerate are to have a yearning desire for the un-
adulterated teaching of the Word of God, the sweet-
ness of which they have already tasted.

4. To draw near unto Christ, the foundation
stone of the great spiritual temple, of which they are
the living stones (2:3-10). The believers collectively
form one great temple (Eph. 2:20-22) of which they
themselves are the priesthood, and where they offer
up spiritual sacrifices. (Compare Heb. 13:10, 15.)
The relation Israel bore to God as an earthly people,
they—Gentiles—bear to Him as an earthly people, for
they are a chosen people, a holy nation, God's own
peculiar treasure (v. 9, compare Deut. 7:6).

5. To live a blameless life, so as to disarm the
prejudice and enmity of the heathen surrounding them.
2:11, 12.

6. To submission.

(a) Submission of all Christians to the government (2:13-17). "It was a lesson so deeply needed
by the Christians of the day that it is taught as em-
phatically by Peter as by Paul himself. It was more
than ever needed at a time when dangerous revolts
were gathering to a head in Judea; when the hearts
of the Jews throughout the world were burning with
a fierce flame of hatred against the abominations of
tyrannous idolatry: when Christians were being
charged with 'turning the world upside down'; when
some poor Christian slave led to martyrdom or put to
the torture might easily relieve the tension of his soul
by bursting into Apocalyptic denunciations of sudden
doom against the crimes of the mystic Babylon; when
the heathen in their impatient contempt, might willfully interpret a prophecy of the final conflagration as
though it were a revolutionary and incendiary threat;
and when Christians at Rome were, on this very ac-

count, already suffering the agonies of Neronian persecution."—Farrar.

(b) Submission of slaves to masters (2:18-25). Servants are to be obedient even to unjust and harsh masters. In suffering injustice silently they will be glorifying God, and they will be true followers of Christ, who did not defend Himself but committed His cause to God the righteous Judge.

(c) The submission of wives to husbands (3:1-7). Christian wives might be led to consider their heathen husbands as inferior to themselves. They are rather to obey their husbands, so that, if the latter will not accept the written Word or believe the spoken testimony, they may be won by the silent and effective testimony of a holy life. In so doing, Christian wives will be following the example of holy women of old.

7. To brotherly love. vv. 8-12.

8. To patient endurance of wrong (vv. 13-16). If they are doing good they have nothing to fear (v. 13). But if it happens that they do suffer innocently they are to remember that a blessing is promised to those who suffer for righteousness' sake (v. 14, compare Matt. 5:11, 12). Inward holiness of heart, and an outward readiness to defend their faith in the spirit of meekness, together with a good conscience would finally make the heathen ashamed of their false accusations (vv. 15, 16). In the matter of suffering unjustly, the believer has the example of Christ, who, as the sinless One, suffered for the unjust. But His sufferings were followed by triumph and exaltation. In triumph, for He proclaimed His victory in the underworld; in exaltation, for He is now seated at the right hand of God (vv. 18-20). In like manner will the Christians' sufferings be followed by glory.

III. Suffering with Christ. Ch. 4.

1. Death to sin (4:1-6). As Christ died to an earthly life and rose again to a heavenly, Christians are to consider themselves dead to the old life of sin and

alive to a new life of holiness (vv. 1-3, compare Rom. Ch. 6). The heathen wonder at their manner of life, and speak evil of them. But right will finally triumph at the time when the Lord shall judge the living and the dead (vv. 4-6).

2. Conduct in view of imminence of the Lord's return. vv. 7-11.

3. The glorious privilege of suffering with Christ (vv. 12-19). Christians are not to be surprised at God's process of testing and refining by suffering, but rather to rejoice in the fact, that they are partakers of Christ's sufferings (vv. 12, 13). To bear Christ's reproach is a sign of spiritual grace resting on them, but to suffer as an evil-doer is a sign of disgrace (v. 15). Let believers expect suffering, for judgment must begin at the house of God—there must be a time of purging and purification for the church. Therefore let those who suffer commit themselves unto Him who is faithful (vv. 17-19).

IV. Concluding exhortations. Ch. 5.

1. To the pastors. Ch. 5:1-4.
2. To young men. vv. 5, 6.
3. To the church in general. vv. 6-11.
4. Salutations. vv. 12-14.

SECOND PETER

Theme. First Peter deals with a danger without the church—persecutions; Second Peter, with one within—false doctrine. The first was written to encourage; the second, to warn. In the first, Peter is seen fulfilling his commission to "strengthen the brethren" (Luke 22:32); in the second he is seen fulfilling his commission to shepherd the sheep, leading them past lurking and insidious dangers, to walk in the paths of righteousness. John 21:15-17. In the second epistle, the writer gives a graphic description of the false teachers who would threaten the faith of the Church, and as an antidote to their false doctrine and tainted life, he exhorts the Christians to avail themselves of every means for growing in grace and in the experiential knowledge of Jesus Christ. The theme may be summed up as follows: a full experiential knowledge of Christ is the stronghold against a false teaching and an unholy life.

Why Written. To give a prophetic picture of the apostasy of the last days, and to urge upon Christians that preparedness of heart and life which alone can fit them to meet its perils.

When Written. Probably A. D. 66.

Contents

     I.   Exhortation to Growth in Divine Grace and Knowledge. Ch. 1.

    II. Warning Against False Teachers. Ch. 2.

  III. Promise of the Lord's Coming. Ch. 3.

I. Exhortation to Growth in Divine Grace and Knowledge. Ch. 1.

1. Salutation (vv. 1, 2). The grace and peace that Peter asks for the saints should issue in experiential knowledge of God and of Christ.

2. The basis of saving knowledge—the promises of God (vv. 3, 4).

3. The growth in experiential knowledge (vv. 5-11). There is no standstill in Christian experience, there must be either progress or falling back. The believer has a foundation, faith; but he must be continually building on that foundation a superstructure of Christian character and virtue. Notice—

    (a) The result of this spiritual "addition" (v. 5): fruitfulness in experiential knowledge of Divine things and the acquiring of an abundant entrance into the kingdom of the Lord Jesus (vv. 8, 10, 11).

    (b) The result of neglect of spiritual growth—spiritual blindness and backsliding (v. 8).

4. The sources of saving knowledge:

(a)   The testimony of the apostles who were eye witnesses of Christ's glory (vv. 12-18).

(b)   The testimony of the prophets (vv. 19-21). "Moreover the apostle appeals to the inspiration of the prophets in the confirmation of his teaching: 'No prophecy of Scripture is of private interpretation. For no prophecy ever came by the will of man: but men spake from God, being moved by the Holy Spirit.' He recognizes this as a primary truth, that prophecy is not of one's own origination, nor is it to be tied up to the times of the prophet. The prophecy was brought to him as it is brought to us. Peter and his fellow-believers did not follow cunningly devised fables; they were borne along in their prophetic utterance by the Holy Spirit."

II. Warning Against False Teachers. Ch. 2.

1.   The conduct of false teachers (vv. 1-3). They will stealthily and cunningly introduce fatal heresies, even denying the Lord Himself. Covering their true motives with plausible arguments they will lead many astray.

2.   The certain doom of these false teachers as set forth by ancient examples of retribution. vv. 4-9.

3.   The character of these false teachers (vv. 10-22). The apostle probably has in mind the future rise of Gnostic sects, who combined tainted morals with tainted living. The following sects arose in the second century: the Ophites, who worshiped the serpent of the Garden of Eden as their benefactor; the Cainites, who exalted as heroes some of the vilest characters of the Old Testament; the Carpocratians who taught immorality; the Antitactae, who regarded it as a duty to the supreme God to violate the Ten Commandments on the ground that they were promulgated by a wicked mediating angel.

III. Promise of the Lord's Coming. Ch. 3.

1.   Scoffers and the promise of the second coming (vv. 1-4). "Presumptuous skepticism and lawless

lust, setting nature and its so-called laws above the God of nature and revelation, and arguing from the past continuity of nature's phenomena that there can be no future interruption to them, was the sin of the antidiluvians (those living before the flood), and shall be that of the scoffers in the last days."

2. Answers to their objections. vv. 5-9.

(a) "They obstinately shut their eyes to the Scripture record of the Creation and the Deluge; the latter is the very parallel to the coming judgment of fire. . . . 'All things continue as they were from the beginning of creation.' Before the flood the same objection to the possibility of the flood might have been urged with the same plausibility: the heavens and the earth have been from old. How unlikely then that they should not continue so! But, replies Peter, the flood came in spite of their reasonings; so will the final conflagration of the earth come in spite of the scoffers of the last days."

(b) God's delays are due to His mercy.

3. The certainty, suddenness, and effects of the Lord's coming (vv. 10-13). The "day of the Lord" here mentioned refers to a whole series of events beginning with the premillennial advent and ending with the destruction of the wicked and the final conflagration and general judgment. "As the flood was the baptism of the earth, eventuating in a renovated earth partly delivered from the curse, so the baptism by fire shall purify the earth so as to be the renovated abode of the regenerated man wholly delivered from the curse."

4. Concluding exhortations:

(a) To live blamelessly in the light of their great Hope. v. 14.

(b) To remember that reason for the Lord's delay is to give men an opportunity to repent (v. 15). Paul himself has written concerning the second Advent. Many, who are unstable in faith and shaken by every seeming difficulty, hastily misinterpret difficult texts in his writings, instead of waiting for God by His Spirit to make them plain (v. 16).

(c)   To beware of being led astray by false doctrine. v. 17.

(d) To grow in grace. v. 18.

CHAPTER XI

FIRST JOHN

Theme. The **Gospel** of John sets forth the acts **and** words which prove that Jesus is the Christ, the Son of God; the **First Epistle** of John sets forth the acts and words which are obligatory upon those who believe this truth. The Gospel deals with the fundamentals of Christian faith; the Epistle, with fundamentals of Christian life. The Gospel was written to give a foundation of faith; the Epistle, to give a foundation of assurance. The Gospel leads us across the Father's threshold; the Epistle makes us at home in the Father's house. The Epistle is an affectionate letter from a spiritual father to his children in the faith, in which he exhorts them to cultivate that practical godliness which brings perfect fellowship with God, and to avoid that type of religion where actions do not conform to profession. To accomplish his purpose the apostle lays down a number of rules whereby true spirituality may be tested—rules that draw a rigid line of demarcation between those who merely profess to walk in love and holiness and those who really do so. Though John is plain-spoken and severe in dealing with erroneous doctrine and inconsistent living, yet on the whole his tone is affectionate and shows him as deserving of his title "the apostle of love." The frequent recurrence of the word "love" and the form of address "my little children," makes his epistle breathe an atmosphere of tenderness. The following story concerning John will not be out of place in this connection. It is said that when the apostle had arrived to an extreme old age and could with difficulty be carried to the church in the arms of his disciples, and was too weak to give any lengthy exhortations, he would say no more at their meetings than this: "Little children, love one another." The disciples and fathers wearied of this constant repetition of the same words said, "Master, why dost thou always say this?" He replied, "It is the Lord's command, and if only this be done, it is enough."

We shall sum up the theme as follows: the grounds of Christian assurance and of fellowship with the Father.

Why Written. It was written for the following purposes, as stated in the epistle itself:

1. That the child of God might have fellowship with the Father and the Son, and with one another (1:3).

2. That the child of God may have fullness of joy (1:4).

3. That he may not sin (2:1).

4. That he may recognize the grounds of his assurance of eternal life (5:13).

When Written. Probably about A. D. 90.

Where Written. Probably at Ephesus, where John lived and ministered after leaving Jerusalem.

Contents

I.   Introduction.   1:1-4.

II.   Fellowship with God.   1:5 to 2:28.

III. Divine Sonship.   2:29 to 3:24.

IV.   The Spirit of Truth and the Spirit of Error. 4:1-6.

V.   God Is Love.   4:7-21.

VI.   Faith.   5:1-12.

VII. Conclusion: Christian Confidence.   5:13-21.

Note. The quotations in this study of John are from Pakenham-Walsh's Commentary on 1 John (McMillan Co., New York).

I. Introduction. Ch. 1:1-4.

1. The substance of the Gospel: the deity, incarnation of Christ.   v. 1.

2. The guarantee of the Gospel:

Light

(a) The apostle's experience (v. 1). They had come into personal contact with the Word of life.

(b) The apostolic testimony. v. 2.

3. The purpose of preaching the Gospel. v. 3.

(a) That believers might have fellowship with the apostles and all Christians.

(b) That the believers might share in all the blessings and privileges that the apostles had gained from their fellowship with the Father.

4. The result of the Gospel: the fullness of joy that comes from perfect fellowship with God (v. 4).

II. Fellowship with God. Chs. 1:5 to 2:28.

The apostle lays down the following tests of fellowship with God.

1. Walking in the light (1:5-7). "There were false teachers in John's days, who were trying to induce Christians to leave the church and join their heretical body. Among other things, they taught that if a man's mind were enlightened with heavenly knowledge, it did not at all matter what his conduct was like; he might commit as much sin as he pleased. John says that such doctrine would overthrow all holiness and truth, and was utterly opposed to Christianity. So he makes it very clear in this section that, far from its being true that all conduct is alike to the enlightened man, it is the character of his conduct that will show whether he is enlightened or not." God is light; i. e., He is the fountain of pure truth, pure intelligence, pure holiness. He who is walking in the darkness of willful sin, lies when he says that he has fellowship with such a Being.

2. Consciousness and confession of sin (1:8 to 2:1). To claim sinless perfection, or, on the other hand, to deny the sinfulness of certain bodily acts (as did the Antinomians) is to deceive ourselves and to give the lie to God's revelation. It is God's will that we should not sin. When God's light reveals sin in us we are to confess it and obtain that cleansing

old/new citizenship

which the blood of Jesus and His intercession for us
makes possible.

3. Obedience to God's commands in imitation of
Christ (2:2-6). "The false teachers maintained that
knowledge was the one and all-important thing; if a
man were enlightened with what they considered the
knowledge of love, it did not matter how he lived.
John wishes to show that such knowledge is a delusion;
that all true knowledge of God must result in holiness
of life, otherwise it is a dead and useless thing. He
therefore bids men test their knowledge of God, and
if they want to know for certain whether they have
the knowledge of God, the test is simple—do they
keep God's commandments?"

4. Love to the brethren (2:7-11). John is writing an old-new commandment; old, because they heard
it when they first became Christians; new, because it
is fresh and living to those who have fellowship with
Christ, the true Light now shining for them.

5. Unworldliness (vv. 12-17). A Christian cannot love God and love the world at the same time
—the world, disordered by the unrestrained prevalence
of sinful forces and fettered in the bondage of corruption.

6. Pure doctrine (2:18-28). The believers have
heard of Antichrist who will come at the end of this, the
last age. But his spirit is in the world at the present time
in the person of certain false teachers who deny the
Deity and Messiahship of Christ. The Christian
need not be led astray by the subtle and plausible arguments of these errorists, for the Spirit would lead
them into all truth. "There is an undoubted allusion
here to a false teacher, Cerinthus, who denied that Jesus was the Christ and held that the man Jesus and the
aeon or spirit, Christ, were distinct beings. He taught
that Jesus was an ordinary man till His baptism when
this 'aeon' descended upon Him, gave Him the power
of working miracles and revealed to Him the hitherto
unknown Father. This aeon, being incapable of suf-

fering, left Jesus before His passion. Hence the two central truths of the incarnation and the atonement were denied by this teaching. . . . These false teachers were continually saying to the Christians, 'You have need of a great deal of instruction; follow us and we will lead you into the depths of Christian faith. We know the hidden mysteries and can teach you who have need of teaching.' John reminds the Christians of their anointing, of the presence in their midst of the divine Teacher, the Holy Spirit. . . . Having the Holy Spirit, they needed no other teacher, and they might boldly claim this unction in the face of the haughty teachers of error. He does not mean to say that they needed no Christian teacher, no instruction from the lips of an apostle or teacher in the church. (See Eph. 4:11; Heb. 5:12.)

III. Divine Sonship. Chs. 2:29 to 3:24.

The following tests of divine sonship are laid down by John:

1. A righteous walk (2:29 to 3:10). The Christian is to show an absolute antagonism to sin because of the following facts:

(a) His divine sonship and the hope of becoming like Jesus. 2:29 to 3:1-3.

(b) Sin is lawlessness (transgresssion of the law)—in essence, rebellion against God. 3:4.

(c) Because of Christ's character and His atoning work for us (vv.5-7). So far as we abide in Christ we do not sin; so far as we sin we do not abide in Christ.

(d) Because of the diabolical origin of sin. v. 8.

(e) Because of the God-begotten quality of the Christian life. v. 9.

(f) Because the final test as to whether we are children of God or children of the devil lies in our actions. v. 10.

2. Love to the brethren. 3:11-18.

(a) The command. v. 11.

(b)   The warning.   v. 12.
(c)   The consolation.   vv. 13-15.
(d)   The pattern.   v. 16.
(e)   The practical illustration.   vv. 17, 18.   "Actions speak louder than words."
3.   Assurance.   3:19-24.

(a)   The basis of assurance.   v. 19.   The practice of God-inspired love toward the brethren, and not only our feelings which are variable, is the test of the reality of our faith and our union with Christ.

(b)   The results of assurance.   vv. 20-24.

IV. The Spirit of Truth and the Spirit of Error.
     Ch. 4:1-6.

The thought of the Spirit dwelling in us (3:24) leads John to treat in a parenthesis of other spirits— false and evil spirits and how Christians may distinguish them.

1.   The appeal (v. 1).   However eloquent and gifted a prophet may be, his teaching is to be tested.

2.   The test (v. 2)—the confession of Christ's incarnation.   "This all has a special bearing on our own days, when there is so much heard of spiritualism, theosophy, and the communications of men with spirits and with the spiritual world. . . . The test proposed by John may be applied as surely and certainly today as ever; there is **one** 'medium' of spiritual communication between the invisible and the visible world, between heaven and earth, that is **Jesus Christ come in the flesh.** All true spirits will unite themselves to Him; all untrue ones will deny, setting themselves up (whether they are clothed in human bodies or not) as independent mediums, creating intercourse between heaven and earth."

3.   The conflict (v. 4).   There had evidently been a conflict between Christians and false teachers, but the Church had adhered to the truth.   Their victory is our victory today.

4.   The contrast (vv. 5, 6).   Those possessed

by the Spirit of God attract disciples similar to themselves, earnest men filled with spirit and doing righteousness; the others attract disciples similar to themselves, worldly men whose lives are evil.

V. God Is Love. Ch. 4:7-21.

1. The call to love. v. 7.

2. The reason for love: "God is love." v. 8.

3. The proof of divine love: God's sacrifice. vv. 9, 10.

4. The claim of love: God's love toward us calls for love on our part toward our brethren. v. 11.

5. The result of love on our part: the manifestation of God's presence (vv. 12-16); boldness (v. 17); absence of condemning fear (v. 18).

6. The proof of our love: the proof of our love for the invisible God is the love for our brother who is made and renewed in God's image (vv. 19-21); the proof of our true love for the brethren is found in our love for God (5:1, 2); our love for God finds its manifestation in the keeping of His commandments. (v. 3).

VI. Faith. Ch. 5:4-12.

1. The victory of faith (5:4, 5) "And this is the victory that **overcame** (the Greek has the past tense) the world." "John uses great boldness in speaking of the victory as past. In each believer there is a power of life from God, exercised by faith which must conquer, which from God's point of view has conquered. In the body of believers, the church of God, there is the same power for the ultimate conquest of the world. When John wrote, the church was a despised, insignificant sect, consisting chiefly of slaves and poor low-caste people; it was far from perfect; it was vexed with false teachers; the world was the solid, united, irresistible heathen power of Rome, commanding all the wealth, the strength and resources of civilization. And yet John not merely prophesied that the church would conquer the world, but asserted that

it had done so. And further his words imply that the complete conquest of all the evil that remains in ourselves, of all the evil that exists in the world, of every system of falsehood or wickedness which fights against God, is assured, and fiom the divine standpoint accomplished."

　　2.　The threefold earthly witness of faith.　vv. 6-8.

　　(a)　The water witnesses to the beginning of Christ's earthly ministry inaugurated by His baptism.

　　(b)　The blood witnesses to His death which brought eternal redemption.

　　(c)　The Spirit witnesses in all ages to His resurrection and endless life.

Notice the emphasis in verse 6; "not by water only, but by water and blood." Cerinthus, John's chief opponent, taught that the heavenly Christ descended upon Jesus at His baptism but left Him on the eve of His passion; so that Jesus died, but the Christ, being spiritual, did not suffer. That is, that Christ came by **water** (baptism), but that he did not come by **blood** (death). The apostle's object is to prove that He who was baptized and He who died on Calvary was the same person.

　　4.　The heavenly witness.　vv. 9-12.

VII. Conclusion: the Christian Confidence. Ch. 5: 13-21.

　　1.　The substance of the Christian confidence— the assurance of eternal life.　v. 13.

　　2.　The manifestation of Christian confidence.

　　(a)　Outwardly the power of offering effectual prayer.　vv. 14:17.

　　(b)　Inward conviction—"We know."　vv. 18-20.

　　3.　Concluding exhortation (v. 21).　"In Jesus you have found Him who is the true God and eternal life.　If you are in Him that is true, you are bound carefully and earnestly to make a complete chasm between yourselves and all heathen things, and now shun the idols which you once worshiped."—Schlatter.

SECOND JOHN

(Read the epistle)

Theme. The **first** epistle of John is a letter to the Christian family in general, warning against false teaching and exhorting to practical godliness. The **second** epistle is a letter to a particular member of that family, written for the purpose of instructing her as to her attitude toward false teachers. She was not to show hospitality to such. Such an injunction may sound harsh; but it was justified on the grounds that the doctrines of these teachers struck at the very fundamentals of Christianity, and in many cases menaced purity of conduct. By receiving such in her house, the believer to whom John was writing would be identifying herself with their errors. John did not mean to teach unkind treatment of Christians who happen to differ from us doctrinally, or of those ensnared by error. He was writing at a time when Antinomian and Gnostic errorists were attempting to undermine the foundation of faith and purity, and under such conditions it was imperative that Christians denounce their teachings both in word and in attitude. The theme may be summed up as follows: the duty of obeying the truth and avoiding fellowship with its enemies.

Why Written. To warn a hospitable Christian lady against entertaining false teachers.

THIRD JOHN

(Read the epistle)

Theme. This short epistle gives us a glimpse of certain conditions that existed in a local church in John's time. The story which may be gathered from the epistle seems to be as follows. John had sent out a band of itinerant teachers with letters of commendation to the various churches, one of which was the

assembly to which Gaius and Diotrephes belonged.
Diotrephes, either from jealousy for the rights of the
local church or for some personal reason, refused to
tender hospitality to these teachers and excommunicated those members of his church who received them.
Gaius, one of the members of the church, refused to
be intimidated by this spiritual autocrat, and enter-
tained the repulsed and disheartened missionaries, who
later reported his kindness to the apostle. It seems
that John was about to send forth a second time these
teachers (v. 6) and he exhorts Gaius to continue in his
ministry of love toward them. John himself wrote
a letter of remonstrance to Diotrephes, which was
ignored. Therefore the apostle expressed intention
of paying a personal visit to the church and of depos-
ing this ecclesiastical tyrant. We shall sum up the
theme as follows: the duty of hospitality toward the
ministry, and the danger of domineering leadership.
   Why Written. To commend Gaius for entertaining those Christian workers who were entirely de-
pendent on the hospitality of believers, and to denounce the unhospitable, tyrannical attitude of Diotrephes.

JUDE
(Read the epistle)

   Theme. There is a certain resemblance between the second epistle of Peter and that of Jude;
they both treat of apostasy in the church and describe
the leaders of that apostasy. Concerning this subject
it seems that Jude quotes from Peter. (Compare 2
Peter 3:3 and Jude 18.) They both have in mind the
same class of errorists—men of loose morals and
shameful excesses. Peter describes the apostasy as
future; Jude, as present. Peter sets forth the false
teachers as godless and extremely dangerous but not
at their worst; Jude, as depraved and as lawless as they
can be. It was the presence of these men in the church

and their activity in spreading their pernicious doctrines that led Jude to write this epistle, the theme of which is: the duty of Christians to keep themselves spotless and to contend earnestly for the faith, in the midst of apostasy.

Authorship. The author is believed to be Jude the brother of James and of our Lord. Mark 6:3.

Why Written. To warn them against apostates within the church, who though having denied the faith still retained their membership.

When Written. Probably between A. D. 70 and 80.

Contents. The following is a brief analysis of the epistle:

After the salutation (vv. 1, 2) Jude mentions the purpose of his writing. At first he had intended to write concerning doctrine, but the presence of false teachers had caused him to sound out a warning to believers to contend for the truths of the Gospel (vv. 3, 4). To illustrate the doom of these teachers three examples of ancient apostasy are given (vv. 5-7). These apostates, ever yielding to their own sinful fancies, are guilty both of fleshly sin and of rebellion against authority (v. 8), and speak of authority in terms that Michael the archangel did not dare to use in speaking to Satan (v. 9). They dare to speak evil of spiritual things about which they are ignorant; yet in the things they do understand they corrupt themselves (v. 10). Their sin and their doom is prefigured by Scripture (v. 11) and by nature (vv. 12, 13). They are the true subjects of Enoch's prophecy (v. 14). As to character, they are complainers and murmurers, scheming flatterers, mockers of spiritual things, men who bring divisions, and who are utterly fleshly, having not the Spirit of Christ (vv. 16-19). But believers, in contrast with these are to build themselves up in the faith, pray in the Holy Ghost, abide in God's love, ever looking to Jesus (vv. 20, 21). In regard to those in error they are to have compassion on those weak ones who have wavered; others they are to save by desperate effort, but always watching lest they be contaminated with the filthy garment of tainted doctrine and sensual living (vv. 22, 23). Jude concludes with a Doxology well suited to the subject he has been discussing—a doxology that praises Him who is able to keep the believer from falling into apostasy and sin, and who is able to keep him blameless until the great Day (vv. 24, 25).

CHAPTER XII

THE REVELATION

Theme. The book of Revelation is the climax
of God's revelation of truth to man, the capstone of
the edifice of the Scriptures, of which Genesis is
the foundation stone. The Bible would not be complete without either book. If the omission of Genesis would have left us in ignorance as to the begin-
nings of things, the omission of Revelation would
have deprived us of much light concerning the consummation of all things. Between Genesis and
Revelation a striking balance may be seen, as follows:

GENESIS	REVELATION
Paradise lost.	Paradise regained.
The first city, a failure	City of the redeemed, a success.
The beginning of the curse.	No more curse.
Marriage of first Adam.	Marriage of second Adam.
First tears.	Every tear wiped away.
Satan's entrance.	Satan's doom.
Old creation.	New creation.
Communion broken.	Communion restored.

The book of Revelation is the consummation
of Old Testament prophecy. It is full of symbols
and language borrowed from the writings of those
prophets who were favored with glorious revelations concerning the end-time—Isaiah, Ezekiel,
Daniel and Zechariah. It is the grand "Amen" of,
and the glad "Hallelujah" for, the fulfillment of the
predictions of the prophets—the glad answer to
their yearning and prayer that the kingdom of God

might come and that His will might be done on earth as it is in heaven. "As the completion of the whole prophetic Scriptures it gathers up the threads of all the former books and weaves them into one chain of many links which binds all history to the throne of God."

Above all, this book is a revelation—an unveiling—of the Lord Jesus Christ. In his Gospel, John describes His earthly life and ministry. Before writing the book of Revelation, the apostle is caught up to the throne of God where he sees the Lord Jesus clothed with the glory which He has with the Father before the foundation of the world; where he sees Him who was judged by the world, returning as its Judge; where he sees Him who was rejected by men, taking possession of all the kingdoms of the world, as King of kings, and Lord of lords.

The Revelation is the book of Christ's coming in glory, therefore we shall sum up the theme as follows: The coming of Christ in glory, as the supreme climax of the age.

Why Written. It was written by John the apostle at the direct command of Jesus, in order that there might be a book of prophecy for this dispensation.

Where Written. On Patmos, an isle off the coast of Asia Minor, about A. D. 90.

Contents. The analysis of 1:19 will give us the three main heads of our outline:

I. Concerning Christ: "The things which thou hast seen." Ch. 1.

II. Concerning the church: "The things which are." Chs. 2, 3.

III. Concerning the Kingdom: "The things which shall be." Chs. 4-22.

Facts to be remembered in studying Revelation:

1. The book is confessedly the most diffi-

cult of interpretation of all the books in the canon. One has said, "His courage is greater than his wisdom who finds no room for doubt in the interpretation of much in the Apocalypse." In meeting some portions the meaning of which is not clear, rather than seek for strained, fanciful and far-fetched interpretations, it is better to say, "I do not understand," and then wait patiently for light.

2. It is quite probable that the interpretation of the book will become clearer as time arrives for the fulfillment of its prophecies. In Old Testament times, the coming of the Messiah was a fact agreed upon by all the pious of the nation; but to them, Messianic prophecy must have presented many difficulties of interpretation, as the book of Revelation does to us. Even the prophets did not always understand their own prophecies. 1 Peter 1:10, 11. It was as the prophecies concerning the Christ began to be fulfilled that the spiritually enlightened among the people—of whom Simeon (Luke 2:25-35) is an example—would find their perplexities disappearing as the rays of the "bright and morning Star" would shine on the pages of sacred Writ. We can all agree as to the main facts of the book—coming tribulation and judgment, the coming of Christ in glory, the setting up of His kingdom, etc.—and then wait patiently till further study, increased spiritual enlightenment and passing events shed light on those details which at present seem obscure.

3. Apart from the interpretation of the book, there are many valuable lessons to be learned, many warnings to be heeded, many promises to encourage, that make the book of Revelation of real practical value to the Christian. For example, the messages to the churches contain practical teaching that can be applied both to the church and to the individual. In this connection it is well to remember that it is always more profitable to

practice the things that we do understand, instead of puzzling, speculating, and splitting hairs over the things that we do not understand.

4. Since the book of Revelation is a mosaic of Old Testament prophecies and symbols, the study of certain prophets—Isaiah, Ezekiel, Daniel, and Zechariah—will provide the key to many a closed door in its interpretation.

I. Concerning Christ: "The things which thou hast seen." Ch. 1.

1. The introduction. vv. 1-3.

(a) Note the correct title of the book, "the revelation (unveiling) of Jesus Christ."

(b) The means of communication (v. 2). The Lord "signified" it; i. e., communicated it by means of signs or symbols.

(c) The blessing to the reader, hearer and the keeper of the sayings of the book. v. 3.

2. The salutation (vv. 4, 5), from—

(a) The Father. v. 4.

(b) The seven Spirits; i. e., the Holy Spirit in His diversities, power and operation. v. 4.

(c) From Jesus Christ. v. 5.

3. The praise. vv. 5. 6.

4. The proclamation—the coming of Christ. vv. 7, 8.

5. The Prophet. vv. 9-20.

(a) His mood, "in the Spirit."

(b) The time of the vision, "on the Lord's day."

(c) The place, the isle of Patmos.

(d) His vision. "It is well that our memory should dwell much upon the Christ who lived and walked as the Son of man upon this earth, but this scene in Revelation is a picture of the Christ of to-day. It is the picture of the Christ who sits on the right hand of God in glory. This is the coming Christ. This is the Christ we think of as we wait and look for His coming. And what a figure!

The Spirit ransacks the realm of nature for symbols that might convey some faint conception to our dull and finite minds of the glory, splendor, and majesty of the Coming One, who is the Christ of Revelation."—McConkey.

II. Concerning the Churches: "The things which are." Chs. 2, 3.

The churches mentioned in these chapters actually existed in John's day and the conditions prevailing there then called forth the Lord's message to them. But these local churches are evidently a type of the entire church and therefore the messages may be applied to the church in every age, as shown by the following facts: the number, seven, is clearly typical, for there were more than seven churches in Asia Minor in John's time. "Then, too, mark the space given to them. The book of Revelation is so terse and so condensed that but one chapter is given to the millennium, and less than one to the advent of Christ. That these two chapters here, comprising ten per cent of the book, should be given over to messages to the seven churches bespeaks the wider scope of the messages."—McConkey.

In studying these chapters we shall notice the following facts concerning each church:

(a) A message of commendation.

(b) A message of rebuke.

(c) A symbolic title of Christ suited to the needs of the church.

(d) A promise to the overcomers.

(e) A historical reference that will cast some light on the message.

1. The message to the church at Ephesus. 2:1-7.

(a) Commendation: works, patience, abhorrence of false teachers.

(b) Rebuke: spiritual declension.

(c) Title of Christ: to a church which has lost

its first love He is one walking in the midst of the seven candlesticks—a superintendent subjecting their works and motives to a severe scrutiny.

(d) Promise to overcomer: tree of life.

(e) Historical reference. Ephesus has been called the "Vanity Fair" of Asia. It was a wealthy, cultured, corrupt, and idolatrous city, the center of the cult of Diana, to whom a magnificent temple had been erected.

2. Message to the church at Smyrna. 2:8-11.

(a) Commendation: endurance in persecution.

(b) There is no message of rebuke to this suffering church.

(c) Title of Christ: to a church facing persecution, the Lord reveals Himself as the One who suffered, died and rose again.

(d) Promise to overcomer: deliverance from second death.

(e) Historical reference. "I will give thee a crown of life." The "crown of Smyrna" was a circular street consisting of a ring of magnificent buildings. One of their philosophers advises them to value more a crown of men than a crown of buildings.

3. Message to the church at Pergamos. 2:12-17

(a) Commendation: faithfulness in testimony.

(b) Rebuke: the prevalence of licentiousness and idolatry.

(c) Title of Christ: to a church tainted with immorality and idolatry He is the One who will fight against it with His two-edged sword.

(d) Promise to overcomer: hidden manna.

(e) Historical reference. Pergamos was the center of idolatry, and had a great altar erected to the worship of a serpent god. This may explain the words "where Satan's seat is."

4. Message to the church at Thyatira. 2:18-29.

(a) Commendation: charity, service, faith.

(b) Rebuke: toleration of corrupt teachers.

(c) Title of Christ: the One with eyes as a

flame of fire (see v. 23), and One with the feet like brass (symbolical of judgment).

(d) Promise to overcomer: power over nations.

(e) Historical reference. Thyatira was a prosperous city celebrated for its trade guilds. Membership in one of these guilds conferred many privileges. Perhaps there is a warning here to Christian tradesmen not to join themselves to pagan brotherhoods and thus participate in idolatrous customs (v. 20).

5. Message to the church at Sardis. 3:1-6.

(a) Commendation: works (though imperfect).

(b) Rebuke: spiritual deadness.

(c) Title of Christ: to a church spiritually dead, He is One holding the seven stars—churches —in His hands, and also the seven Spirits of God, the power of which is able to quicken those churches.

(d) Promise to overcomer: clothed in white raiment and name confessed before the Father.

(e) Historical reference. "I will come upon thee as a thief." Sardis was the scene of the final overthrow of Croesus, the great Lydian king, when the Persians attacked the city. In the year 546 B. C., thinking himself absolutely safe in his citadel which he considered impregnable, the king neglected to set a watch. Finding an unguarded spot, where the rain had washed away a cleft in the soft rock, the Persians climbed up one by one and captured the city. Thus by one night of carelessness the great Lydian empire fell.

6. Message to the church at Philadelphia. 3:7-13.

(a) Commendation: obedience to Christ's commands and steadfastness in testimony.

(b) Rebuke: there is no direct reproof, although "the faint praise of a 'little strength' has in it the shadow of a rebuke."

(c) Title of Christ: to a church eager to enter the open door of missionary service, Christ is the One who has the keys that open doors no man can shut.

(d) Promise to overcomer: pillars in God's temple; a new name.

(e) Historical reference. At one time Philadelphia was destroyed by an earthquake, and so terrified were the inhabitants ever afterwards that they lived outside the city in huts and booths. "Him that overcometh will I make a pillar in the temple of my God (in a building which no earthquake can shake), and he shall go out no more (as the people did during the earthquake). Later the city was built at the expense of the Roman government, and was given a new name, this last signifying that the city was consecrated in a special way to the service and worship of the emperor. "I will write upon him my new name." However, the city later dropped its new name.

7. Message to the church at Laodicea. 3:14-22.

(a) Commendation: praise is lacking for this church.

(b) Rebuke: spiritual lukewarmness.

(c) Title of Christ: to a lukewarm church, unfaithful in testimony, He sets Himself forth as the Amen, the true and faithful witness.

(d) Promise to overcomer: to share Christ's throne.

(e) Historical reference. Laodicea was a wealthy and prosperous city. Following an earthquake, when other cities were accepting imperial help, it declared its independence of such assistance. It was "rich" and had "need of nothing." It was celebrated for the manufacture of a soft black wool, and for costly garments which were made from it

(v. 18). It was celebrated throughout the Roman empire for its school of medicine, and for the "Phrygian powder" from which its well-known eye-salve was made (v. 18).

III. Concerning the Kingdom: "The things which shall be." Chs. 4 to 22.

1. The vision of God's throne (Ch. 4). The prophet is caught up, in spirit, to the throne of God, and from there—from the viewpoint of the heavenlies, he is made to see the judgment that will be poured out upon the earth in the latter times.

2. A vision of the Lamb (ch. 5). The main feature of this chapter is the unsealing of a book handed to the Lord. In discussing the nature of this sealed book, Mr. McConkey says: "What is the symbolism of a seal? A seal may be indeed used to attest the signature to a title-deed. But it is also used to conceal and safeguard the contents of a written document. We seal a letter for that purpose. In prophecy God uses the seal in precisely this way. He tells Daniel (Dan. 12:4) concerning certain prophecies which are to be hidden that he is to "seal the book." He tells John concerning the very prophecies of Revelation which He wants disclosed to His servants "seal not the sayings of the prophecy of this book." Rev. 22:10. This use of the seal therefore to conceal the prophetic word seems to be the clear and natural usage here with the seven-sealed book. . . . In it the scroll of New Testament prophecy is unrolled by Jesus Himself as He breaks the seals in their divinely appointed order."

3. The seals (Chs. 6 to 8:1). The author quoted above raises the question as to whether Revelation has a story thread, or a story-flow, and whether Christ ever told the Revelation story before. He then points out that the seals constitute

the story thread of the book, and that their message resembles closely that of Christ's discourse
recorded in Matthew 24. Another scholar, Milli-
gan, takes the same view. Following the suggestions of these men, but not their exact outlines,
we offer the following parallel:

Matthew, Ch. 24	Revelation, Ch. 6
False Christs (24:5).	First seal
War (vv. 6, 7).	Second seal
Famine (v. 7).	Third seal
Pestilence (Death) (v. 7).	Fourth seal
Tribulation (v. 21).	Fifth seal
C e l e s tial disturbances (v. 29).	Sixth seal
Second advent (v. 30).	Seventh seal

4. We have then seen that the seals represent
the very backbone of Revelation. But what is the
relation of the trumpets and the vials to the seals?
The explanation given is that they do not run
parallel, but the seventh seal expands into the seven
trumpets, and the seventh trumpet expands into the
seven vials. Mr. Graham Scroggie holds the same
view, explaining these sections on the principle of
inclusion, the seven trumpets being included in the
seventh seal, and the seven vials in the seventh
trumpet.

5. In following the story-flow of Revelation, the
student will notice that we have passed over certain
episodes. This has been done because these do not
form part of the story thread, but are detached from
it. Mr. McConkey refers to these as "insets." For
example, in examining a map of a state, we may see
in a corner a map of a certain city in that state.
This is an inset, giving a "close-up" view of the
city. Or in a picture of a famous battle, there may
be given in the same space pictures of special portions of the battlefield, or portraits of famous

generals who took part in the campaigns. So in Revelation, the writer passes along rapidly, describing the course of events that terminate in Christ's coming, but here and there he stops to give us a "close-up" view of some particular personage, company, or city. Of such we may notice the following:

(a) Two companies, a Jewish and a Gentile. Ch. 7.

(b) The angel and the book. Ch. 10.

(c) The two witnesses. Ch. 11.

(d) The two wonders. Ch. 12.

(e) The two beasts. Ch. 13.

(f) Two pictures of Christ—the Lamb and the Reaper. Ch. 14.

(g) Babylon. Chs. 17, 18.

6. Having noticed the main story thread of Revelation, and the parentheses, we shall sum up the conclusion briefly:

(a) The second advent. Ch. 19.

(b) The millennium. Ch. 20.

(c) The new heavens and the new earth. Chs. 21, 22

Notes

Notes

Notes

Notes

Notes

Notes

Notes

Notes

Notes

Notes

Notes

Notes